**Survival
in the Wilds**

OTHER BOOKS BY CHARLES K. FOX

Advanced Bait Casting
This Wonderful World of Trout
Rising Trout
Armchair Adventure for the Angler
Gettysburg

Survival in the Wilds

Robert O. Shockley
and
Charles K. Fox

South Brunswick and New York: A. S. Barnes and Company
London: Thomas Yoseloff Ltd

© 1970 by A. S. Barnes and Co., Inc.
Library of Congress Catalogue Card Number: 73-112767

A. S. Barnes and Co., Inc.
Cranbury, New Jersey 08512

Thomas Yoseloff Ltd
108 New Bond Street
London W1Y 0QX, England

I SBN 0-498-06968-0
Printed in the United States of America

This Book
Is Dedicated to
Those Who Regard Open Space as an
Irreplaceable and Important Resource
and One Essential to
Quality Living

Contents

	PREFACE	9
1	STATE OF MIND	15
2	FIRST AID	20

Resuscitation — Heart Attack — Snakebite — Gila Monster — Insects — Contact Plants — Diarrhea and Dysentery — Scurvy — Fever Blisters — Clothes Bandages — Sprains — Fractures — Heatstroke — Sunstroke—Heat Exhaustion—Fire and Sunburn — Frostbite — Severe Bleeding — Shock — Fainting — Object in Eye — Hygiene — Nature's Dangers

3	ORIENTATION	39

Discovering One's Directions — Cardinal Directions — Stars — Finding Direction with a Watch — Directions by Compass — Alone in Camp — Seeking the Truth — Keeping Contact

4	SIGNALING	45

Smoke Signals — Mirrors

5	WATER AND ITS SUBSTITUTES	49

Importance of Water — Running Water — Swamp Water — Elemental Water — Water Table — Beach Wells — Indicators of Water — Dew Water — Snow Water — Ice Water — Fiords — Water from Fish — Water from Plants—Sheep Flukes—Alkali Water—Purification of Water — Filtering Water

Survival in the Wilds / 8

6	FIREMAKING	60
	Basic Principles—Flint and Steel—Bow and Drill—Hand Spindle — Vine and Fiber — Magnifying Glass — Gunpowder — Spark Plugs and Exhaust — Draw-String Method — Reflector — Torches — Lamps — Miscellaneous Points — No Fire	
7	IMPLEMENTATION	71
	Cutting Edges — Hand Drill — Bow and Arrow — Spears — Sling — Bola — Canteens — Quarter Staff —Writing Materials — Goggles — Snowshoes— Basketry — Pottery — Soap Making — Preparing Animal Hides — Tanning — Fishing Equipment	
8	HUNTING	96
	Large Game — Small Game — Birds — Crustaceans — Mollusks — Turtles and other Foods	
9	PLANTS	105
	Mushrooms — Fruits — Beverages from Plants — Bark as Food — Starvation — Special Plants and Fibers—Yucca—Palms—Testing Plants for Toxicity	
10	COOKING AND PRESERVING FOOD	115
	Bread Oven — Turtles — Miscellaneous Cooking — Hobo Stove—Sugar and Salt—Preservation of Food— Jerky — Smoked Meat and Fish — Pemican — Pinole — Salting — Blanching	
11	SHELTER	125
	Para-Tepee — Lean-to — Hogan — Adobe — Caves	
12	TRANSPORTATION	133
	Boats — Canoe — Toboggan — Eskimo Boats — Dugouts — Travois — Water Travel — Jellyfish Float	
13	TRAPPING	141
	Traps and Snares	
14	THE SURVIVAL KIT	144
	Check List — Firearms	
INDEX		149

Preface

During Robert O. Shockley's wilderness explorations, including those with the distinguished naturalist, Dr. Cahn, he was keenly aware that nature can be kindly or harsh. It is manifestly clear that a person who knows little about the ways of the wild may perish, the ultimate price to pay for ignorance of the mechanics of survival, whereas another who has acquired knowledge about nature and is schooled in the art of survival will thrive. While drawing from your own resources and the natural resources about you, it is possible to make nature your friend and protector; thus it is that under primitive circumstances knowledge makes the difference between life and death.

The threat of "the bomb," bacteriological warfare, and gas has ushered in a day of survival-consciousness which calls for preparedness on a nationwide scale. It is both practical and patriotic to be ready, because such preparedness is a deterrent to a foe and solace to a friend.

Today, more people than ever before venture into the wilds and out-of-the-way places, getting close to nature. Many are just ordinary people—hunters, fishermen, picnickers, nature lovers, prospectors, and the like. Some are men of science, such as naturalists, archaeologists, geologists, explorers—who deliberately or inadvertently are confronted with the forces of nature. But there is one fact to bear in mind, however disorientated or lost one may become: every need will be supplied to those who are armed with an understanding of what nature has to offer.

Included in this book are facts which might be considered as mined nuggets to be passed on to others. The contents will provide a useful body of knowledge. These are not untried theories; they have been practiced first hand by Robert O. Shockley, a missionary, in circumstances closely associated with Mother Nature.

This book is intended not only for the strong and the fit; it is for people of all degrees of health, strength, and endurance regardless of lack of experience or skill. It seeks to equip anyone with the requirements of survival if they use the principles and techniques that have been ruggedly tested and proved effective.

It has been asked by people throughout history what unseen force draws men into primitive places. Some are motivated by wanderlust and a desire to blaze new frontiers; others merely want to get close to nature. Whatever the urge, it is like a contagion that causes people to leave wealth, comfort, and loved ones. Many are lost through accident, ignorance, or sheer carelessness; and so there is need for a practical, compact guidebook.

Thousands become lost, stranded, planewrecked or shipwrecked every year in the United States, not only in Canada, Mexico, the other Americas, and other countries.

In civilized areas we more or less take life for granted. But sustaining life on survival status while pitting ourselves against the forces of nature is a supreme challenge.

The strongest instinct in all living creatures is self-preservation, a tremendous will to live. Yet we must adjust ourselves to situations for which heredity and nature have not prepared us.

There is a saying, "Where is life, where works it, where lurks it?" We scarcely detect it, yet it is manifest in many ways.

In a book of ancient laws it is written that "Life is in the blood." "While there's life, there's hope." When the odds are stacked against us, it is of prime importance that we possess and maintain a spirit of hope, fortitude, and confidence, for in order to survive we sometimes have to do things that ordinarily are unthinkable. A necessity like drinking the blood of a freshly killed animal would hardly be resorted to by most people; but it can maintain strength, for blood not only contains moisture but vitamins, salt, and minerals vital to existence.

All in all, we need to have faith and confidence in ourselves besides courage and knowledge, for who knows but that the next time we enter a forest, desert or swamp, all of which have attractions, beauty and splendor, we might be lost amidst the unrelenting harshness of nature. At such a time we require all the faith, self-confidence and will power that can be mustered to keep a steady hand and a cool, clear mind.

Without hardware, grocery or drug stores at hand, a person must supply his vital needs from whatever nature offers in the way of resources.

Survival techniques are actually means of substitution, such as making fire without matches (of which there are a number of ways), hunting, trapping, fishing, and foraging in order to take food from Mother Nature's vast foodlocker. There are times when it is necessary to purify water or to tap water substitutes in order to subsist. Also, there is the matter of shelter from harsh elements; clothing can become an acute problem, especially in the extremes of weather conditions.

This book can teach you how to arm and equip yourself by simple, effective means. It tells you how to traverse the highways of the wilderness, the rivers. It tells you how to recognize edible wild plants and how they can be used. It offers instruction on how to orientate yourself in strange surroundings, how to maintain health and composure while seeking a way back to camp or home. This is a book about problems and their solution.

I know people who, because of the rocket and the hydrogen bomb threat, carry two or three weeks' supply of food and water in their cars. This meager supply would soon vanish after serving them for only a limited time and need. What then?

With the means described here, an individual or a group of individuals can be sustained not just for days or a week, but for an extended length of time—perhaps indefinitely.

Survival under the most adverse circumstances is yours for the reading.

Charles K. Fox
and
Robert O. Shockley

Survival
in the Wilds

1
State of Mind

A proper state of mind is of paramount importance to a person or persons during a crisis when the elements expose human life to danger. It will be to one's advantage if he possesses knowledge of the assets which increase the possibility of survival. One should have an observing eye for things that are of significance to survival. What may be obscure to the untrained eye can spell the difference between survival or death.

When stranded or lost, your survival time will depend on the knowledge and skill at your command and your ability to improvise or draw successfully from natural resources.

When lost, one should give some time and thought to an appraisal of the situation. He should assume a constructive attitude, not a helpless, hopeless one; and he will find that it fills his mind with helpful thoughts that tend to alter things for the better. This greatly increases chances of survival. From self-confidence comes courage; panic and fear will be dispelled. While analyzing the chances for getting oriented, don't be hasty. There is the well-known saying that "fools rush in where angels fear to tread." If you don't plan your course of action, you may be just spinning your wheels, so to speak, getting nowhere. Furthermore, things will almost certainly become complicated. Faulty or foolhardy judgment—that is, taking an unnecessary chance, has often caused grief, or has resulted in spending an uncomfortable time in the woods.

Survival in the Wilds / 16

The survival instinct in all creatures is strong, and if things come to the worst, one will clutch at straws. You can avoid that sort of panic. Death is an ever present threat to one lost in the wild; it lurks and stalks in many forms. It may be simple and subtle or harsh and bold. Death may present itself in the form of dangerous wild animals; exposure to the extremes of sun, wind, lightning, and storms of all kinds; or it may be in the form of quagmires, quicksands, avalanches, ice or snow, field or forest fires, venomous reptiles, hunger, thirst, injury or disease.

Nature must be put to work so as to increase the chances of survival. The first impulse in many, when faced with a difficult problem, is to give up. Just remember that a quitter never wins, and a winner never quits. Of course, no one wants to die and will fight with all his might and main to sustain life in his body in the face of this kind of misfortune.

In what might seem to be insurmountable circumstances, persistence usually pays off. By generating a lot of will power and fortitude, one is usually able to overcome the odds against him. In other words, one can master a situation, overwhelming as it may be, by changing it around or bending it to serve his purpose.

The Boy Scout slogan is a good one to remember and adhere to: "Be Prepared." There are many who would perish with plenty all around, who could save themselves if only they recognized and knew how to utilize the many good things which Mother Nature has provided, free for the taking. Truly, there is no substitute for mental preparation.

This is an old saying: "On the plains of hesitation bleach the bones of countless millions who sighted their goal, and sat down to rest, and resting, perished." Again I say that one must persevere if he is to achieve his goal. Survival is not for the faint of heart—you get out of something only what you put into it.

One thing which can be helpful is to try and dredge up ideas by turning loose your imagination. Writing a thing down or sketching a map often brings helpful hints to mind which bring forth the answer to a problem.

Concentration eliminates haphazardness or guesswork and may help to overcome the difficulty. When fear and panic rush in, away goes composure and ability to rationalize. It is a good idea just to rest if exhausted and if possible take a nap. It can be said that being lost ranges from peace to panic, depending on the person who finds that nature has played him a trick. With the average person it is disconcerting or very unnerving.

Some people who are lost have tried to recall stories they have read or heard related from others' misadventures. Some curse, some repeat a prayer; but whatever you choose to do, think of the things that will help you to acquire self-composure and get the situation in hand. Crowd fear out of your mind and allow no room for it; calmness will replace your anxiety and panic will subside. Faith is the opposite of fear, and hope is the opposite of doubt. Faith and hope will serve you; fear and doubt can enslave you. Fear is a dreadful thing that reduces one's ability to think and formulate a plan. Everyone, especially one who is in trouble, needs to be in good mental trim. Fear of the unknown scares or panics most people. Often, one has to take the known quantity to discover the unknown, and so it is with being lost in wild and unfamiliar country. One should try to pick up threads or clues to where he has been, where he had missed his way, then try to decide which direction to go.

Why not depend on nature to find the direction? Compare

your course with the position of the sun, the location of the stars, the lay of the land, the flow of a stream, or the direction of the prevailing wind. You may observe the inclination of the brush or trees, for prevailing winds may have bent them from the time they were seedlings. This is a common phenomenon in the Western states as the Pacific breeze exerts its prevailing force on the flora of the land. Moss grows on the side of rocks and trees in the direction of the prevailing wind in any given locality. This is also true of lichens. These winds bring moisture and in turn generate greater growth of moss and lichens on the side of rocks and trees where the wind blows constantly.

In Arkansas and neighboring states the rock strata invariably run in a northeasterly, southwesterly direction. In the mountains this rock is frequently exposed to view. This provides a sure way of finding one's bearings. In the northland there is a so-called arrow plant whose leaves point to the north, and one may rely on it to point toward that direction when it is in leaf. Summing up, it can be said that observation plus knowledge can lead you to safety.

Although thousands of persons are lost and rescued every year, some, unfortunately, do not return. In 1961 the explorer son of a well-known American was lost in the jungle wilds of the southwest Pacific. Perhaps if he had taken survival training or had with him a good book on survival methods he would have returned home.

Another man was more fortunate, although he suffered unduly. In 1961 he became separated from his party in Alaska. Although armed with a sheath knife and machete, he suffered many hardships for lack of knowledge that survival training would have given him. He lived off raw fish and berries and almost starved to death. Had he carried with him a book on survival, he could have had his vital needs supplied in the Arctic by applying survival principles.

Some years ago, as a member of a forestry crew in the Cumberland Mountains in east Tennessee, I was working on Norris Lake, where it was my job to clear debris from along the lake shore because it would float out from the banks and wreck speed boats.

At this time, it so happened, the coal miners from atop the mountain went on strike and had no means of making a regular livelihood. Many families moved down to the lake and set up housekeeping in the outjutting rock shelters and caves along the water's edge. At night they took along their miner's lamps and devised ways and means to catch fish. During the day they hunted the forests and fields for wild game. With what little money they could afford they bought essentials, including flour, coffee, salt, and cooking oil. These were rationed out among themselves. Also, to supplement their scant food supply, they picked wild greens and gathered chestnuts and berries. They drank from the clear mountain springs and from the lake that bordered their sancutary. These people had no real conveniences or luxuries but they were a happy and contented lot during those months of dire need.

And so it is, survival is yours if you have the key that opens the door to it.

Remember:

> Life's battles do not always go
> To the stronger or faster man,
> But sooner or later the man who wins
> Is the man who thinks he can.

2
First Aid

First aid may be defined as any correctly administered treatment given to a sick or injured person before professional medical help is obtained. It commences with a steadying effect, when a stricken person realizes that competent hands will help him. New problems arise at the outset when a person is injured or stricken with illness, especially when it happens suddenly. Events may seem unreal, if not remote, to the suffering person. Often he is unable to think clearly. The emotional reaction associated with a serious or severe accident subsides only gradually. Therefore, first aid is more than applying a splint to a fracture or dressing to a wound. It relates directly to the victim's mind and spirit or sense of well-being, as well as to his physical injuries. A word of encouragement, an expression of readiness to help, and the evidence of the first-aider's capability has an elevating effect on the patient.

A skilled first-aider will invariably deal with the entire situation, the patient and his ailments. He knows what not to do as well as what to do. Thus he avoids the errors so commonly made through well-meant but misguided efforts. The skilled one sticks only to what is necessary to treat the victim and yet keeps the handling of injured parts to a minimum.

THE VALUE OF TRAINING

Many people learn first-aid methods in order to help others, but it is of primary help to the student himself. Besides making him become safety-conscious, it enables him to treat himself in time of need. Also, if incapicated beyond self-help, he may be able to direct others to help him. Thus he need not entrust his injured body to the ministrations of a random passer-by. Knowledge of first aid sharpens one's desire always to take precautions and adhere to safety measures when faced with a dangerous situation. It focuses attention upon special ways to avoid trouble and accidents.

When accidents are of a minor nature, the first aid indicated will be obvious to the trained first-aider. But for urgently needed first aid, which goes from serious to severe to critical, there is a sequence of action to be taken. First, one should give the urgently needed first aid which usually calls for the victim to lie down; then, one should check for injuries and plan what to do and from that point on carry out the indicated procedures.

In many cases, first aid can be the most important part of treatment a victim gets. One should have a basic knowledge of it before venturing into wild and desolate parts of the country. Also, training in rescue work is of value when the occasion arises.

Urgently needed first aid should be given promptly. One should act quickly and deftly where each second of delay is important. Although discussed more fully in following pages, a few of the more serious kinds of accidents will be mentioned, such as (a) severe bleeding, (b) stoppage of breathing where artificial respiration is needed, and (c) poisoning.

While the first-aider's time and attention is devoted to the injured person, someone else should summon help, certainly a doctor if one can be obtained.

Survival in the Wilds / 22

RESUSCITATION

Figure 1 illustrates the mouth-to-mouth method which has proven to be the most effective treatment for victims of drowning, electric shock, or when the breath is knocked out of a person. It is included also in treatment for heart attack and as such is considered by medical experts to be effective.

Figure 1. MOUTH-TO-MOUTH RESUSCITATION

While applying this method to victims, proceed as follows. One or two persons may bring the victim out of water, face up, with a third person starting resuscitation at once by placing his mouth over the mouth of the victim, *then* while breathing twice as deeply as normally, blowing his breath into the mouth of the victim. When this is done, all the oxygen is not burned up and there is enough for both persons. Water can be removed from the victim's stomach by lowering his head and turning it to the side and then pressing on his stomach. This causes the water to pour out the victim's mouth.

One should make sure that the victim has not swallowed his tongue or has some foreign object in his mouth, such as mud, chewing gum, or false teeth. If two persons are available, one should hold the head behind the victim's jawbones and pull forward so as to clear tongue blockage from the air passage. If no one else is on hand to assist, hook your index finger over his lower teeth, pull the jaw forward, and hold it in this position, with finger in the corner of his mouth. Close the nostrils by pinching with the free hand to prevent the air from escaping through his nose. Now breathe deeply, and after putting your mouth over his, exhale deeply into victim's mouth. This will expand his lungs. Repeat this action until the victim recovers or until a doctor arrives to take over. The face and nails of the victim may turn bluish or black, but when new life is breathed into him his complexion will regain its pinkish color.

It is most important that this treatment be continued even if there is no sign of recovery or until rigor mortis sets in. Some victims have revived after two hours of such treatment. Warm blankets or coats should be kept over and under the victim, with his head lowered.

HEART ATTACK

The above treatment should be given to a victim of heart attack if two persons are on hand. While the one does this, the other should face the victim, who is flat on his back. He should place one knee between victim's legs and place one hand directly over victim's heart with the one hand on top of the other; then press quite hard and release suddenly in rapid succession (about seventy times a minute). Such hand pressure will push the blood out of the heart chambers into and through the arteries. Continuous treatment stimulates a continuous flow of blood to all parts of the victim's body; or, in other words, it simply starts circulation artificially. A pink color will return when the victim is revived. The treatment should be continued. Always take patient to a doctor if possible, or better yet, bring the doctor to the patient.

SNAKEBITE

In countries where poisonous snakes are common, one should develop "snake sense." If you keep alert, especially in climbing steep slopes, around the water's edge, or under bushes located in or near the water, while stepping over logs or rocks or when wandering through fields and woods where foliage is thick, you will probably avoid snakebite. Besides being careful where you walk, you should be very careful where you put your hands when picking anything off the ground, and take precaution when you sit or lie down on the ground. Trouser legs are no protection against most snakes; a second covering is needed. Not all boots are foolproof protection. However, trouser legs are adequate protection against the coral snake, as it has short teeth and it fastens on and wriggles or "chews" before injecting venom. This requires several seconds. On being bitten by this snake one should quickly tear it loose by grabbing and pulling.

Snakes are just as afraid of you as you are of them and usually bite when molested or stepped on or taken by surprise. They want nothing better than to be left alone.

Snakes can strike at a distance of two-thirds their length. Of course, one should have a healthy respect for them. Never pick up or play with a snake unless you know it is harmless.

Poisonous snakes may be encountered during the daytime, especially during a dry season, when seeking water, because where there is water there is food. Snakes move in the late autumn in search of a place to hibernate. Remember, generally snakes are camouflaged by color and markings that blend with their natural surroundings. Be especially careful where snake food is plentiful. They prey upon fish, frogs, insects, rodents and other small animals, and birds' eggs.

Nonpoisonous snakes leave a bite mark shaped like a horse shoe. It should be treated with antiseptic as you would any scratch or wound. Venomous snakes leave two puncture marks made by their two fangs, and sometimes their smaller teeth leave scratch marks. The bite will burn like fire. Swelling is immediate. This is the time to keep calm and cool, but act quickly and as deftly as you can. Do not panic, for this accelerates the heartbeat, which in turn spreads the poison all the more rapidly.

Fatalities are caused by false sense of security or by inadequate first-aid treatment. Actually, only one-tenth of one percent of snakebite victims die.

There is an old but mistaken notion that a piece of raw snake or raw chicken applied to the bitten area will draw out the poison. This is pure hokum and should never be resorted to. Since most victims do not die, ignorant people attribute the saving of life to the raw-meat treatment. Alcohol is bad medicine for snakebite; it only speeds up circulation.

Experts agree that the most effective treatment for snakebite is suction, either by use of rubber cups or by mouth and lips. If the mouth method is used, be sure that you don't have any sores or bad teeth in your mouth. Wash your mouth out from time to time during and after treatment.

The first step is to make the victim lie down and cut a cross mark with a sterile (flame-heated) blade over each fang mark. The cuts should be one-quarter inch deep or less, and one-quarter inch long. Then moisten the area and apply the suction cup. If the bitten area is covered with hair, it may facilitate suction by shaving the area with a well-honed knife.

Now apply a tourniquet or ligature one inch above the bite. This should be only tight enough to slow down the flow of lymph just under the skin, but not so tight as to slow or obstruct the flow of blood in the deep arteries. You need to draw some blood, but not very much, and the constriction band or ligature should be released for thirty seconds every ten to twenty minutes to prevent gangrene from setting in. This occurs when the blood dies from lack of sufficient oxygen. Cut shallow cross marks at the edge of the swelling as it progresses. Always cut lengthwise to the arm to help absorb and dilute the poison. Too much loss of blood weakens the victim and causes shock. Fifty to one hundred cross marks may be necessary.

Most snakebite treatment is insufficient rather than overdone. A good antiseptic, such as iodine, should be applied to the cuts and to the fang marks before suction is begun. This is very important because bacilli from the rattlesnake's mouth may complicate the condition with serious infection. Also, the victim should be treated for tetanus. As swelling progresses, remove the constriction band to an inch above it. A neckerchief, belt, piece of clothing or rope will do to encircle the limb and should always be tied between the bite and the heart.

Snake venom is both neurotoxic (destructive to nerve tissue) and hemotoxic (destructive of blood cells). Antivenin assists in neutralizing the neurotoxins, and the hemotoxins are removed by mechanical means such as a suction cup. One should try to identify the snake so as to match it with the proper antivenin. However, an antivenin has been developed that is effective for practically all venomous snakes.

Coral snakes are identified by their black, yellow, and red ring bands. They are among the most deadly snakes found in the United States; the venom paralyzes the nerves and respiratory system. Copperheads, moccasins, and rattlesnakes affect the blood stream as the poison coagulates the blood.

Except for the coral, most of the harmless snakes have bullet-shaped heads. Copperheads, moccasins, rattlers have angular heads and are poisonous. The teeth of coral snakes are one-eighth inch long, where as other three named poisonous snakes' fangs are three-eights, five-eights and three-quarters of an inch respectively. Besides having movable, hollow fangs, they have a lateral pit on the side of the head between eyes and nostrils.

Treatment may be helped additionally by using ice or rags saturated with cold water to pack around the bitten area, which tends to retard the flow of lymph.

Remember, all snakebite victims should be treated for shock. A good substitute treatment is to give the patient a quart of water with a level teaspoon of salt dissolved in it. Also, it is beneficial to make an application of Epsom salts to the bitten area by applying it on a wet cloth.

The gila monster has orange and black beaded areas on the body and is cousin to the beaded lizard of Mexico. These are the world's only two poisonous lizards and they rarely bite humans. Although they appear to be slow and sluggish, they can move and bite quickly and hold strongly. One should not approach or molest these reptiles. Play it safe by taking no chances with reptiles and snakes.

Snakebite kits may be obtained at sporting goods, hardware and drug stores. Some drug stores in Florida rent or sell kits for $20 and up.

INSECTS

Mites, chiggers, and ticks can be real pests and one should take measures to avoid them or to treat their bites. Mites and chiggers can be discouraged by dusting one's clothes with sulphur or by eating cream of tartar tablets. These sweat out and cling to the skin, which creates a deterrent to biting insects. After going through brush and weeds infested with chiggers, one may take a bath with strong soap and use rubbing alcohol rubbed in well, soon after being exposed. You may leave the soap suds on your body for two hours before washing it off, so that the lye in the soap can kill the chiggers.

Rocky Mountain spotted fever ticks are somewhat longer in body than are the ordinary wood ticks and they can transmit fever or infect one with a fever which may be fatal. A doctor should be summoned if you are ever bitten by this species of tick.

Ticks may be removed when fastened to one's body by burning them with a lighted cigarette or with live coals of a fire brand. Also, one may drop oil on the pest and cut off its oxygen. It will soon turn loose and emerge for air.

Scorpions, centipedes, tarantulas, and black widow spiders inflict an extremely painful bite, but rarely fatal. Their venom may be removed by means of a cross cut and suction cup. Antiseptic should be applied to the bitten area. Death may result if the victim's condition is poor.

Bee, wasp, yellow jacket, and hornet stings may be relieved by mud, ammonia, or soda.

Mosquitoes can be driven off by dense smoke of an open fire. Good repellents are made by smoking red cedar or its bark, green fern leaves, or peppermint weeds. This is done when store-bought repellents or mosquito dope is not available.

While traveling in mosquito-infested areas, avoid wearing

light-colored clothing, especially white, as these attract more mosquitoes than do dark clothes. Incidentally, according to scientific testing, light-colored clothes reflect up to seven degrees of heat.

Mosquito bites should be treated by washing with hot water and strong soap.

CONTACT PLANTS

Besides watching for poisonous snakes and insects, one should be able to recognize poisonous plants. The most common are the poison oak and the poison sumac, which have white clusters of berries. The red sumac, whose red berries are harmless, should not be confused with the poisonous sumac. An adage concerning poisonous plants is, "When the leaves are three, let it be." Actually this refers more specifically to the poison ivy and the poison oak.

Do not inhale the smoke of these plants when they are burning. If you happen to brush against a contact plant you should immediately wash the affected area thoroughly with warm water and strong soap and then apply alcohol. The toxic property is alkaloid found in all parts of the plant. The plants are most poisonous when the sap is rising in the spring.

DIARRHEA AND DYSENTERY

These are transmitted through contaminated food or drinking water. Either may be checked by drinking tannic acid made by boiling red oak bark, acorns, or bark of the hemlock tree. Also you may drink a solution of water and pulverized burned bones or pulverized limestone.

SCURVY

Scurvy can be prevented or cured by eating wild fruits or boiling the needles or bark of the pine and spruce or of conifers in general.

FEVER

When one is affected with a fever, he should lie quiet and drink liquids from time to time and keep cool by bathing. A rich broth is often good.

BLISTERS

If you get a blister on your feet, it should be left unbroken and then soaked in hot water. If it has burst, apply a strong antiseptic and after washing it with hot water and soap, bandage it. Animal suet (tallow or fat) will help keep it soft.

Care of feet is important as they need to be in good condition for traveling. In the wilds you are only as good as your feet.

CLOTHES

If your shoes or trousers are too tight, stand in water for a few minutes and then wear them until dry. This stretches them and makes them form-fitting.

BANDAGES

Bandages may be made of cattail fluff, strips of parachute, spreads or bands of leather, strips of bark or cloth. Cattail fluff serves as cotton, which tends to keep out impurities and is easily flushed off with soap and warm water.

Bandages can be sterilized by boiling or by scorching over hot coals.

Cuts and scratches may require only a good disinfectant but should be washed out thoroughly if dirty.

SPRAINS

Treat sprains and bruises by applying ice or cold compresses or cold running water for the first twenty-four hours and then change to hot water. Salt or Epsom salts are helpful. Walking on a sprained ankle is encouraged but, of course, that depends on the severity of the pain.

One may make a rather serviceable crutch by cutting a bush with a forked branch and a side limb at hand level. When trimmed of its branches, the fork may be padded out to fit under the armpit. The bottom end of the crutch should be pointed so as to insure traction in any type of terrain. Two such crutches will greatly facilitate movement.

FRACTURES

Fractures may be simple or compound. Those having bones which puncture the skin are called compound fractures. They should be cleaned and disinfected before setting and bandaging. If someone is on hand to assist, have him pull the broken limb straight out with a hard, steady pull until the splintered bones align and adjust. After this is done, bandages and splints should be applied.

An injured person may be carried on a travois, as described in the chapter on implementation.

A good stretcher or litter can be made by using two stout poles with the poles slipped through the sleeves of two coats, or by wrapping a blanket around the poles so that the patient can lie on the last fold of the blanket, to keep it from unfolding. Leather skins, strings or leather or bark can be woven around the poles to form a couch.

HEATSTROKE

Lack of salt in the blood is a prime cause of heat stroke or heat exhaustion. Muscle stiffness is reduced if one gets plenty of salt. Too much, however, has an adverse effect. In warm climates salt is lost beyond the danger point of evaporation unless you get an extra amount in your food or drinking water. If salt is unavailable, a few swallows of sea water a day will help to replace your needed quota. It will not hurt you if plenty of fresh water is drunk and it will relieve a tired, sluggish feeling.

While traveling in the sun on hot days, a cap of cloth or leaves is better than no cap at all. One should not travel without head protection. An Arab-type headdress and neckcloth are necessary in some climates. Also, a cloth should be worn over the face while traveling in heat or over sand or snow.

Don't overexert yourself during hot periods of the day, especially if you are in a weakened condition. Sometimes you can cool off by splashing in water with your clothes on. The resulting evaporation will keep you comfortable.

SUNSTROKE

Sunstroke is the result of direct exposure to the sun. It may come upon you suddenly, but is usually preceded by dizziness, nausea, and headache. The face will be flushed, the skin will be hot and dry, and the body temperature runs high. A good preventive measure is to keep your head covered and drink plenty of water with ample supply of salt in it. Wetting your clothing will help. For treatment, lie in the shade with the head elevated. Bathe the head and body and get plenty of rest.

HEAT EXHAUSTION

This comes from long exposure to high temperature and high humidity, with or without the sunlight. Symptoms differ from those of a sunstroke. The skin is clammy, with body temperature about normal or below. Lie in the shade and drink salt water. Keep the head lower than the body and remain covered in order to keep warm.

FIRE AND SUNBURN

Burns and scalds can be of first, second, and third degree. A first-degree burn reddens the skin and is accompanied by pain. Most sunburns are of first degree. With second-degree burns, blisters form. Extreme care should be exercised to prevent the blisters from breaking and admitting germs. Serious complications result if infection sets in. With third-degree burns some skin may be burned away and some of the flesh is charred. This destroys growth cells which form new skin. If a burn covers a large area you can be certain that shock will set in, so give first aid for shock as well as treating for the burn.

In treating first-degree burns you may apply a solution of tannic acid by boiling bark of red oak or hemlock. A thin layer of animal fat (oils) or coconut oil will help to alleviate the pain. Better still, to further reduce the pain, hold the burnt area in cold running water until pain subsides.

If blisters form, you are up against a more serious burn. Do not apply ointment. Protect blisters by covering them with sterile bandages or gauze. Give the patient plenty of fluids.

Third-degree burns are the most severe. Do not try to remove clothing, as it may be sticking to the flesh. Bear in mind that shock is surely present. If handy, wrap a clean sheet around the victim and get him to a hospital. If this is impossible, moisten clothes sticking to the burnt area with water that has been boiled and cooled, and remove them gently as they loosen. Ordinarily, ointment should not be used except as might be prescribed by a doctor, but in an emergency with no doctor available, a thin oil is better than nothing, as it keeps the burn soft and prevents drying and breaking of tissue.

Contrary to popular belief, it has been discovered that holding a burnt part in cold water reduces the burning sensation with no ill effects. In case of serious burns, a cold solution of boiled water containing an ample amount of salt solution is good when applied for an extended period of time with a sterilized cloth. Keep this wet until the burn heals. Sulfa drugs may be carried in an emergency kit for treatment of cuts and burns.

FROSTBITE

Frozen face, ears, hands, and feet is an ever-present danger at low temperatures. Cold winds increase the danger of frostbite and one should do as the animals do—seek shelter during severely cold gales. Winds reduce body heat, and a wind at zero can be more dangerous than still weather at a much lower temperature.

Frozen parts should be thawed slowly. Do not rub the frozen part, so that breaking the skin and flesh is avoided. Contrary to popular opinion, never rub frostbitten parts with snow. Frozen flesh is white and stiff, while milder frostbite is pinkish or dark red. The ears are especially susceptible to frostbite. Press your warm hands against them. When fingers or hands become frostbitten, warm them against the bare skin of your body. Dry feathers, grass, moss, or animal fur placed in the shoes help keep your feet warm. Animal fur is good for stockings, face scarf, ear muffs, or mittens. In cold winds, a face scarf should always be worn.

Lowest temperatures occur during clear, still weather; temperature rises during snow storms. Never travel until you become exhausted, either in hot or cold weather. Rest often, and sleep if you feel the need. The cold will awaken you before you freeze. One may dig into the lee side of a snowdrift and sit or lie down on fir boughs for a brief rest and warming. If you get wet in extremely cold weather, build a fire in the most sheltered place at hand; otherwise keep moving until your clothes dry out. Never lie down when wet. Breathe through the nose, so as to warm the air before it reaches the lungs, thus reducing the danger of frosting them. When your body is severely chilled, exercise vigorously and drink lots of hot broth or tea. Plain hot water will help. In regulating a balance between body heat and heat loss, one should keep active when away from the fire and wear proper clothes to compensate.

SEVERE BLEEDING

When severe bleeding results from an injury, keep the patient still, with the injured part higher than his head if possible. First apply finger (digit) pressure to the artery and between the injury and the heart, then apply a compress. Don't use a tourniquet unless absolutely necessary. If one is used, release for half a minute every ten to twenty minutes to prevent gangrene. No stimulants are to be given to the patient.

SHOCK

Every accident is accompanied by shock to a greater or lesser degree. A shock victim is very weak, his face gets pale, his skin is cold and sweaty, and his breathing is shallow and labored. He has chills and sometimes he vomits. The victim usually is dazed and in a serious case may lose consciousness. Shock may come immediately after an accident or hours later.

Keep the patient still, elevate his feet above his head, and keep him warm with blankets, etc., above and beneath him. If the victim is conscious, give him sips of water; not otherwise, for it will strangle him. A level teaspoon of salt dissolved in a quart of water helps to revive a victim in shock. More than a level teaspoon of salt to the quart can be harmful.

FAINTING

Fainting is a condition of the nerves that produces a "blacking out." Fainting is caused by sudden shock, exhaustion, or starvation.

Keep the patient lying down and elevate his feet. A fainting person will snap back to consciousness soon after he lies down. If he fails to come to promptly, there is something seriously wrong. Treat for shock and get a doctor.

OBJECT IN EYE

A foreign object in the eye can be extremely painful and may endanger vision. By blinking the eye, tears will often flush out the object. If this fails, pull the eyelid over the other and try to dislodge the object. If the object can be seen, use the moist corner of a clean handkerchief to wipe it out. Anything more serious requires clean bandage and a doctor.

HYGIENE

All living creatures are subject to the laws of growth and decay. This dictates that we look well to our personal upkeep if we want to be healthy, clean, and enjoy a sense of well-being. This contributes much to our stability and our ability to formulate plans intelligently.

It is best to keep well while on survival status. One can do this by avoiding contaminated food or water, by bathing regularly, resting frequently, taking preventive measures against foot blisters or by treating them properly, and by setting up a comfortable bed. These, among other things, help to insure safety.

In one's personal upkeep, "an ounce of prevention is worth a pound of cure," and "a stitch in time saves nine." Be diligent in personal hygiene, for it elevates morale and may prevent illness and disease. Keeping fit enables one to think clearly and maintains a high mental and physical standard, adding much to the chance of survival.

NATURE'S DANGERS

Everyone should learn what things in nature can harm him. These are more often found in the lower forms of life, especially in the microscopic forms. Deadly amebae are likely to be carried by raw, untreated drinking water. This organism may lodge in the kidneys and cause a severe case of dysentery, at which time blood may be passed in the elimination of waste from the body.

Danger may also take the form of various animals. There are also poisonous reptiles to be shunned, and during weather favorable to them there are pestiferous insects of all sorts. Only a few of the insect genera are poisonous, but even the bites and stings of some of the least dangerous can make a person pretty miserable.

Sometimes bats become rabid and will alight on a victim and sink their needle-like teeth into the flesh. One should be cautious in taking shelter in a cave, which bats frequently inhabit. Numerous people have been bitten in old Mexico, the southwestern United States, and other regions.

Certain small animals are commonly known to become rabid. This occurs from time to time among the dog and cat species. Any animal, large or small, that behaves strangely or shows no fear at your approach should by all means be shunned for this reason. Occasionally, such creatures will attack humans without provocation. In the last stage of rabies, hydrophobia sets in, evidenced by foaming at the mouth.

Whereas most animals and even snakes are as fearful of man as man is of them, the grizzly bear of the Rocky Mountains is an exception. A grizzly will sometimes attack without provocation. Even an old sow with a litter will do so.

Crocodiles will attack on sight if a person is in the water, but will scramble away from a person on land. Alligators are cousins of the ferocious crocodile but will rarely attack humans unless ravenously hungry or when molested.

Rattlesnakes will on occasion fight back and may even crawl toward a person if molested.

One should take every precaution to avoid being bitten by the swarms of insects found in the woods; their bites should be treated promptly against infection.

With a little forethought you can find ways of coping with these unwelcome pests.

3
Orientation

Disorientation, the opposite of orientation, is a state of mental confusion, loss of bearings as to time, place, or identity. Orientation is simply the art of direction finding.

Generally speaking, orientation is, or ultimately can be, the most important factor in survival. Regarding sense of direction, there are two kinds of people. There is the sort who, upon entering a woods or desolate area, invariably takes mental notes of his surroundings and of outstanding features such as mountains, rocks, streams, etc. In a subconscious way he is constantly revising and recording his every change of direction, the distance traveled, and the time involved. This person is an asset to a party in the woods. The other kind blunders into the woods giving heed to nothing. He is of little help to himself or anyone else and is therefore a liability.

The person who takes into account his direction, surroundings, and timing is said to possess a natural and inborn instinct, as is the case with a wild animal.

DISCOVERING ONE'S DIRECTION

If you want to find out where you are, you might climb a tall tree or hill to observe the lay of the land. Search for ridges and their drainage patterns, also for conspicuous landmarks

Survival in the Wilds / 40

that might offer a clue to where you had been before losing your way. If this does not prove useful it might give you a feeling of utter helplessness. If this ever happens to you, don't despair. By all means, try to figure out the points of the compass before pushing on, otherwise you will almost certainly get hopelessly confused.

CARDINAL DIRECTIONS

Remember that your cardinal directions can be taken from the sun or the stars if you don't have a compass. Knowing the general direction of the flow of a stream or the outline of the seashore may set you straight.

Again, be warned that if you panic and move on without a plan you may become your worst enemy. Fear and wild imagination can only get you into a morass.

STARS

The five stars forming Cassiopeia (the big W) are positioned with the center star pointing to the North Star. (See

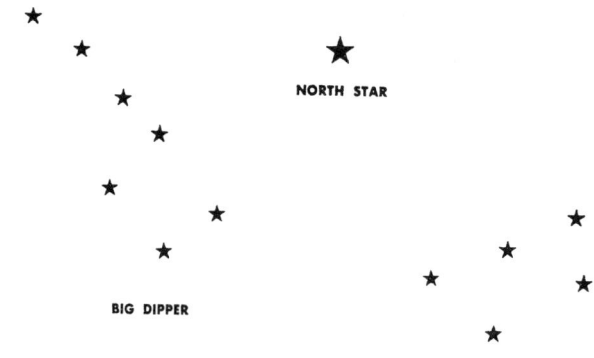

Figure 2.

figure 2.) The North Star is a comparatively small star, whereas to the southwest is the Evening Star, which is large and bright. This star is usually first to be seen in late evening because of its nearness to the earth. It disappears from view soon after dark.

The moon is said to travel from the east to the west. One may face it according to whether it is the first half or the last half of the night, in other words, according to its position in relation to the zenith, then find north. If you face it or the sun in the east before it reaches the zenith, north will be on your left; and when in the west and past the zenith, north will be to your right.

One may refer to the Milky Way or to the Aurora Borealis (Northern Lights) in the Arctic or to the Southern Cross or Aurora Australis in the Antarctic. The Southern Cross is the counterpart to the North Pole.

In the Arctic is a phenomenon called "white out," which is a storm of tiny ice crystals suspended in the air. These particles diffuse the light, and then you are apt to lose all sense of direction. When this occurs, you must rely upon your compass almost entirely. However, a compass is of no use at the earth's magnetic poles.

FINDING DIRECTION WITH A WATCH

A watch which is set to local time can be used to determine the direction. Point the hour hand toward the sun and south will be halfway between the sun and twelve o'clock. This works equally well in the morning or late afternoon. A matchstick or twig may be held upright so that its shadow falls along the hour hand, thus getting you properly aligned with the sun. (See figure 3.) This is especially helpful on an overcast day. This method is of no use near the poles.

Survival in the Wilds / 42

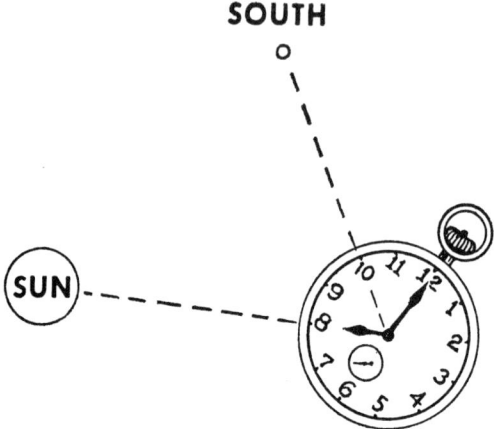

Figure 3. FINDING DIRECTION BY WATCH

DIRECTIONS BY COMPASS

If you are so fortunate as to have a compass and map, you may orient the map. Without a map, you may sketch one if you know the general outline of the country. A map may also be orientated by the sun or stars with close approximation.

To orient with a compass, lay the map flat, place the compass on it, rotate the map until the north-south grid lines are parallel to the compass needle, with the map north (arrow) pointing to or coinciding with compass north. The map is then oriented. This makes all the directions on the map fit those of the earth. To determine the direction you wish to follow, simply place the compass over the spot on the map where you are. A line from the center of the compass to the point of destination will give you the degrees of bearing to be followed. Compass north is magnetic north, and in most areas is not geographic north. Remember that your compass needle will not stabilize if you are standing over a deposit of iron ore or over iron objects. To eliminate this possibility, you must shift your position to an area free of magnetic interference.

If you don't know which direction you should travel, a compass will only enable you to go in a straight line along the selected course.

In densely wooded area without a compass, one tends to go in circles. To overcome this, you should line up three objects such as trees, rocks, etc., and pick up another in line as you pass the first one. Mountain peaks will do as well. Also, one can blaze trees or cut and bend bushes in the direction he is traveling to keep himself in line.

ALONE IN CAMP

If you are alone in camp when the other members of your party are away, you should leave a note of explanation if you leave camp even for a short time. State when you left, where you plan to go, what you expect to do, and when you plan to return. If you happen to get lost, your party will have a good idea how to find you. In such a case it would probably be better for you to just make yourself comfortable and wait for them to come to you. In the meantime, you could be making a smoke signal or other means of attracting attention.

If all else fails, one should proceed downhill, for this usually leads to water and civilization.

Daniel Boone was once asked if he was ever lost. Scratching his head, he thought for a moment and then said, "No, I don't reckin as I ever was, but I was in some mighty strange country for four or five days one time." And as an Indian once said, "Me not lost; tepee lost!"

One should learn the art of orientation, which not only prevents getting lost, but helps to keep one's bearings while trekking through the forest or open country.

Survival in the Wilds / 44

Anyone who roughs it or goes hunting or fishing in the wilds should read this book from time to time until its survival principles become part of him.

SEEKING THE TRUTH

I hope that anyone who reads these pages is able to assume an attitude of skepticism about hearsay methods or theories of finding his way in the woods. The reader ought to discount age-old concepts that are undependable and misleading. For example, it is a timeworn saying that moss grows only on the north side of trees. This is true when referring to the northwoods, but moss indicates the direction from which the prevailing moist winds blow in that locality. Moss on the trees grows thicker on the south side of the trees in the Gulf states; it is denser on the west side of permanent objects in the Western states, since the prevailing wind there comes from the Pacific Ocean, and in turn lays up greater moisture on that side which promotes a greater growth of lichens, algae and moss.

KEEPING CONTACT

Old-timers and woodsmen usually have considerable knowledge about direction-finding and related subjects but have been known to pass on mistaken ideas to the novice. One should always put things to a test and get the proof.

Finally, when two persons or more are traveling through a dense, wooded area, they should use whistles or yell from time to time if they become separated, to keep in contact with one another.

4
Signaling

A knowledge of signal devices is basic when one is thrust into survival status.

Forced to spend an extended period of time in the wilds, one may need to rely on signaling as the only means of rescue and exit, as in the case of illness or injury. With a little ingenuity and searching one can usually come up with at least one effective means of conveying an SOS if an airplane, boat, or traveler comes within range.

One should keep eyes and ears attuned to take advantage of all possible help, and one should keep his signal means handy or readied for immediate use. Conceivably there might be only one chance to use it. Chances of being detected from the air will probably be limited to a short space of time, whereas chances of being seen by boaters, etc., may cover a longer period.

It is universally accepted that three sounds or signals of any sort means distress. These should be investigated on the spot. The signals may be three shots fired from a gun, three posts on the shoreline of a body of water, three rocks, or other similarly arranged contrivance. Repeater-type guns are limited to three shots by law and you may happen to hear a hunter's gun blast in rapid succession. This may simply mean that he has flushed a covey of partridges and that he is just getting off three quick shots. If this is repeated, one might be justified in giving it some thought. However, gun shots intended for signaling should be spaced at fairly close intervals of three at a time. After a while, this should be repeated, but one's supply of shells may make it necessary to economize on shots. When this occurs, it should be interpreted as a distress signal. Don't be abashed at the idea of inquiring; a life might be saved if you follow up by investigating any suspicious incident.

SMOKE SIGNALS

Smoke signals can be made on a hill prominence by using a blanket or coat and smothering the smoke momentarily to collect a puff of smoke before releasing it. Cylinder oil, resinous conifer materials, damp vegetation or green leaves placed in quantity on a hot fire will produce volumes of black smoke, and the intensity of the heat will cause it to rise into the sky unless there is a strong wind. A flame in the darkness may be covered intermittently and at intervals of three at a time, then repeated, as an effective signal at night.

If one is stranded with a motorized conveyance, he should draw gasoline and oil and keep it handy in a container. It can be poured on a pile of brush for lighting a quick fire, thus attracting attention day or night.

MIRRORS

One should carry in his emergency kit two small metallic mirrors of the kind used by the army for signaling. During wartime many a lost soldier has been rescued by the use of this method alone. (See figure 4.) Practice is worthwhile prior to the actual employment of any such device that may save life.

Signaling / 47

Figure 4. SIGNALING BY MIRROR

Signal mirrors can be improvised by fragments of metal from airplanes, boats, or tin cans. One should make a hole in the center of the reflector. It is held about three inches in front of the face, so that a spot of sunlight on the face shines through the hole. This spot will be reflected onto the rear side of the mirror. Now he should maneuver the piece so as to align the reflected spot to coincide with the hole. The mirror can now be aimed directly at the plane or ship.

One may shimmer the mirror by moving it rapidly, so as to cover an area about the plane or boat. This method insures that part of the aiming will coincide with the position of the hoped-for rescuer.

When you are between the sun and a possible source of rescue and you cannot capture the sun's rays in the mirror, you may accomplish it by using two mirrors. This is not at all difficult. All one has to do is to catch the sun's rays on a mirror held on the side of the source of rescue, then bounce the reflection over to the mirror held in the other hand. The mirrors are held about two feet apart. When the second mirror picks up the reflection from the first, it will be in position to reflect a signal to the source of rescue.

Mirrors should be kept in separate cases to prevent marring the surfaces.

One can form the letters SOS in the sand or snow by arranging three boughs, rocks, poles, sea shells or weighted down strips of parachute fabric. Also, one may trample a message in the snow in a conspicuous place and brush out his trail leading to and from it was a bush top.

A constant vigil and a readiness of equipment should be maintained.

5
Water and Its Substitutes

In many parts of the country an abundance of water is to be had from springs, lakes, streams or swamps. I would like to focus attention on getting water in the more inaccessible or difficult places, so that you may learn how to obtain water or water substitutes in any type of terrain.

Life cannot survive long without water, and if any of the following methods is applied in time of desperation it may keep you going until the situation improves. As it is said, "Where there is water, there is life, and where there is life there is hope."

Usually one can find other means of vital necessity wherever water is found, things that will sustain life. Along with water there is usually food obtainable in the form of animals, fish, herbs and fruit; also shelter and fuel.

Chances are good that a time will come when you will need to draw from the contents of this or other chapters if you ever venture close to nature.

Water and fire are tools of unlimited usefulness when harnessed and controlled but may become destructive enemies of the animal and plant kingdom when out of control.

Survival in the Wilds / 50

IMPORTANCE OF WATER

Water is the most important single factor contributing to survival. Food is of little value without it. You can survive many days without food but only a few days without water. Usually about four or five days is the limit of endurance without water, but of course weather conditions make a difference. On a hot, sun-parched desert one may become dehydrated within hours, whereas one might last a week under cool, moist conditions and when activity is kept to a minimum.

A person of average size normally requires at least a quart of water a day. Some people require more than others. A person subject to nervousness will require a good deal more water than the average.

Just carrying a clean pebble, a chip, or hickory nut in the mouth reduces the sensation of thirst. If you are very thirsty and water is found, you should sip it slowly—never drink much at one time. Also, if you are hot, avoid drinking ice-cold water. If you drink a lot of water after getting overheated, you lose a good percentage of it through perspiration. One should sip water more frequently so as to avoid becoming overheated.

Water is a medium that is especially susceptible to conveying germs to humans, especially in tropical areas. If water is drunk from sources near human habitation it should always first be boiled or at least be decontaminated chemically.

RUNNING WATER

Running water tends to purify itself in the sand and sun, but under such circumstances it is not necessarily pure. Conversely, still water is not always impure. Swamp water usually is not stagnant, because of the myriad varieties of plant life

Water and Its Substitutes / 51

which manufacture oxygen and release it into the water, except during dry seasons. This refreshes and sweetens the water constantly.

Sometimes a trickle of water may be found beneath the rocks of an apparently dry creek.

SWAMP WATER

Water found in swamps, although usually dark with decaying vegetation and containing tannic acid from trees, is usually pure and potable so long as streams leading from human habitation do not empty into it. Springs, which form the swamps, usually are safe, especially if they take their source from rocky areas.

ELEMENTAL WATERS

Elemental waters including rain, hail, sleet, and snow are pure, aside from occasions when they might be partly contaminated by radioactive particles.

WATER TABLE

The water table is water collected in the rock stratum of the earth at varying depths and it usually follows the contour of the earth's surface.

Water is often found not too far beneath the surface in low forested areas and river bottoms. Also, it is found along the seashore and desert rivers which seemingly have dried up but actually have only seeped into the sands. Thus water may be obtained by digging.

Survival in the Wilds / 52

BEACH WELLS

Wells that are a few inches to a few feet deep may be dug along the desert streams and a short distance from the seashore. One may dig just above the tide line along the ocean and get water. Here, a well only a foot deep is necessary and the sand provides a filtering action as the water quickly seeps up. Ninety percent or more of the salt and minerals of the sea is filtered out, leaving only a slightly brackish taste, but it is perfectly safe to drink.

INDICATORS OF WATER

In desert lands there are sometimes signs to indicate the presence or nearness of water. Desert birds will lead you to it. Also, game trails converge on a stream or water hole. There are plants which indicate the presence of water nearby.

Some plants thrive only where there is water, either above ground or just beneath the surface. Palms indicate its presence. Rushes, sedges, and the cattail reed are good indicators. Also the elderberry, willow, button willow, and the cottonwood must have a lot of water nearby in order to thrive.

DEW WATER

Dew water can be collected by tapping each droplet into a container or by dragging a cloth through the foliage or grass, and wringing it out. Dew shows up best during nights of clear weather.

SNOW WATER

Snow is a good source of water during the wintertime or

may be found lingering on high mountain peaks in the summer.

ICE WATER

When salt water of the Arctic or the Antarctic seas freezes, the salt separates, leaving pure ice free of salt crystals. This ice is smooth, bluish in color, and good to melt and drink.

In summer, depressions in icebergs and ice floes usually collect lakelets of fresh water caused by snow and rain.

FIORDS

In inlets, fiords and bays, melted sleet, snow and rain accumulates on the surface of the more dense salt water and remains unmixed with the salt water for extended periods of time.

WATER FROM FISH

A fish is one-seventh water. Liquid can be taken from fish by chewing strips of the fillet, by placing strips of the fillet in a rag and twisting until the water exudes freely, or by taking a large fish and making numerous deep gashes in its body, causing the water to seep through the lymphatic glands. You may also eat raw fish and get water that way.

WATER FROM PLANTS

Buds of the palms, especially the coconut and cabbage palms, are filled with succulent juices and may be eaten raw to obtain the stored-up moisture. This is in the form of sugary sap, which provides energy as well as water.

Purslane leaves contain considerable amounts of water and

one can slake a thirst by chewing the leaves and swallowing the juice.

One can notch maple and birch trees in the spring and collect generous quantities of flowing sap.

Cattail stalks have a pith which is filled with water in the springtime (see figure 5). The outer stalk may be peeled off and the pith chewed to obtain water.

The barrel cactus, long used by cowboys and Indians of the Southwest, is a reservoir of watery sap to be had by scalping

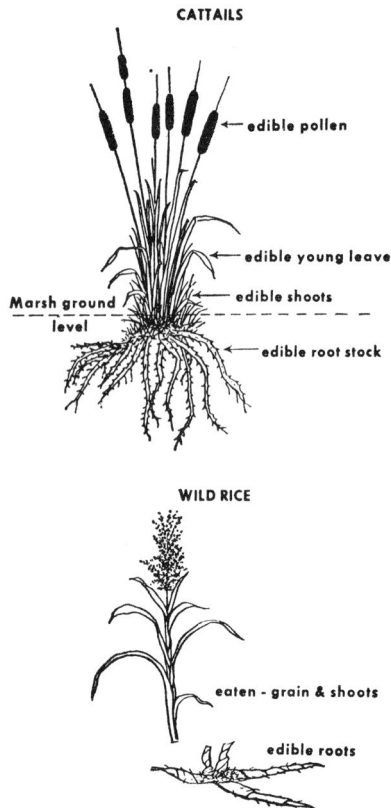

Figure 5.

the top then squeezing the pulp until the sap oozes out. Left alone, it will refill itself. Cactus apples or pears of the prickly pear and giant saguaro cactus contain succulent and nourishing juices and can be rendered more accessible by burning away the tips of the cactus needles or spines.

Tender bamboo and cane shoots can be chewed for their sap; and the mature stems often store water.

Roots of the elm, willow, and cottonwood can be steamed over an open fire, causing the sap to flow. One can also suck the root to obtain moisture. Certain desert plans have roots that contain a good supply of water.

Contrary to popular belief, green coconuts are better than ripe ones. They have a jelly-like substance which affords excellent food as well as moisture.

Many wild plants yield succulent juices containing natural sugars. These fruits afford a good substitute for water when it is scarce.

Air plants which attach themselves to jungle trees (see figure 6) are good water reservoirs and may be stripped of their outer husks and squeezed or chewed raw for their water. These plants are similar to the pineapple in appearance.

Many species of jungle plants collect water in their cuplike leaves or at the base of their frondlike stems. Some may be found in heavily forested areas.

Some trees have knotholes and crotches that collect rain water. This may be discolored, but it is safe to drink except when mosquito larvae are present, in which case it should be filtered and purified by boiling.

Rattans, cross, and grapevines contain water in considerable quantity. One may cut them as high up as he can reach and then cut them at ground level. Always make the topmost cut first, to prevent loss of the sap at the bottom as it flows freely. This can be caught in a container. The weight of the sap can

Survival in the Wilds / 56

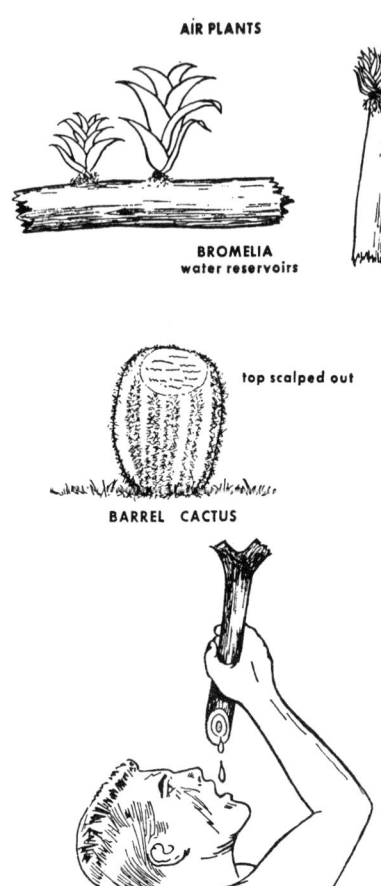

Figure 6.   TAPPING GRAPE VINE

pull the fluid down only to a certain level due to the capillary action of the many tiny tubes in the core of the vine. To overcome this after it has been drained, simply cut the top twelve inches off and it will drain another foot down; then repeat until all has been collected. Fluid from these vines is clear and sometimes has a slightly acid taste. The sap will be much cooler than the surrounding air. If vine sap tastes bitter, don't drink it.

Blades of kelp can be chewed to get water; their gourd also can be drained of water by cutting a small hole at the top and bottom. The flesh-like meat of the gourd itself can be chewed for its moisture. Water from this sea plant may be somewhat brackish but is nevertheless good. Kelp may be seen floating in large masses on the surface of the ocean. One should not overlook the possibility of extracting water from the smaller varieties of seaweed, simply by chewing the stems.

SHEEP FLUKES

Beware of drinking water from outdoor places when in sheep country, as flukes (parasitic worms) transmitted to water from sheep dung will enter your body and can be extremely dangerous. Make a practice of boiling any water whose purity is doubtful.

ALKALI WATER

Alkali water found in desert water holes of the West should never be drunk. It is deadly poisonous. These water holes are recognizable by the lack of vegetation around them. Frequently the bleached bones of unwary animals that drank such water are scattered around. Such a water hole is usually associated with chalky-white alkaloid soil.

PURIFICATION OF WATER

Chlorine is not always dependable as a purifier of water in tropical or semitropical areas, and one should use iodine or else boil the water to make sure of safe drinking.

Iodine should be used in proportions of three or four drops of seven percent tincture per quart of water. Three drops of iodine may be used with one quart of water that is mostly pure, such as mountain spring water. The iodine drops may be reduced when a full gallon of water is used. This should be allowed to set for at least thirty minutes before drinking.

Contrary to the popular notion, freezing water does not purify it of microorganisms. Such water should be treated the same as any other questionable water. Take no short cuts when purifying drinking water.

Naturalists know that desert tortoises have a built-in mechanism for converting desert foliage they have eaten into water, which is stored under the carapace for use during the driest months. These tortoises are *natural walking canteens*, easy to catch, too.

A motorist stranded in a remote desert place can drain water from the radiator for drinking—if it contains no antifreeze. If it is rusty it can be strained through layers of rags.

Springs and pools of water often occur in caves and hollows of lime rocks. This is especially true of caves formed of limestone. Springs in the limestone sections are the greatest in volume, some forming large streams. Such caves are mostly to be found in mountainous areas of the United States.

In the desert one can cool water and render it potable by filling an unpainted vessel of pottery clay and placing it in the shade. The prevailing wind of the desert reduces the heat as the water evaporates and "breathes" through the porous clayware. Also by means of a stout cord, the vessel can be whirled around until the temperature of the water has been reduced. This is the principle of evaporation at work, a cooling process.

A crude but serviceable water filter can be made by upending a section of hollow log or section of bamboo (joint) which has been filled with moss, grass, or sand. A combination of these does the job adequately.

FILTERING WATER

Filtering water doesn't purify it. Filter paper can be purchased and carried in one's emergency or survival kit.

6
Firemaking

When one is in the woods and especially when lost in wilderness areas, it is of utmost importance to know the art of firemaking in case his match supply runs out or gets wet and therefore useless. This can add much to one's security in supplying vital needs.

The various types of lighters are good, but that means you must also carry a fuel supply.

However, the match is usually the most readily accessible means of fire. As most people depend on the match for starting a fire, precautionary measures are necessary to conserve and protect the supply.

Use matches of the sort that burn intensely when struck on a rough surface. Dip a bundle of them head first in liquid shellac, varnish, or lacquer and let them dry. One can depend on these treated matches to strike even if they become wet. However, they should be dried well in the event they do become wet, as they lose their resistance to water when soaked for a few hours.

If these liquids are not available, take paraffin or candle tallow and rub it well over the match head to make it moisture-resistant. This treatment serves very well in cold weather but tends to soften the match head under warm conditions.

As a further precaution, place matches in a small jar or

metal container and, after securing the lid, dip the container in hot liquid paraffin and allow to cool. This seals in the matches—airtight and waterproof.

When lighting a fire, one should have an ample supply of fire tinder or punk, and shield the match from the wind. This should make certain of getting a flame quickly without the loss of a match. Have a supply of wood of graduated sizes and of the proper kind before attempting to build the fire. Anything one does to be sure that each match will work is well worth the time and trouble invested.

Be conservative in your thinking with regard to handling any means to survive. Fire will lengthen your survival time by enabling you to keep warm, cook your food, and destroy harmful germs commonly found in water and food.

It is a good idea to take along leather boot laces for making fire by the bow-and-drill method when all other means fail.

If you practice a few basic principles of fire building, you can always produce fire:

1. Select a dry sheltered place.
2. Use only the driest tinder to start the fire.
3. Have ready a good supply of kindling.
4. Start with a tiny fire and add fuel sparingly at first, as the fire needs oxygen to sustain combustion.
5. Fan or blow the infant flame to a steady increase until the flame can take over on its own.
6. Use dry, dead wood, add green wood later to hold the fire. Afterward a good back log is beneficial in maintaining the fire; it gives greater warmth in cold weather.

In firemaking one should remember that some materials have a lower kindling point than others. These, of course, should be used in starting a fire with those of a much higher kindling point used for back logs.

Although some of the ancient arts have been lost in the process of evolution, the art of firemaking without matches has survived. Doubtless it is because of its vital importance to uncivilized man. Anyone who contemplates traveling to remote areas of the world will do well to learn and practice the ancient and time-proven methods before the need arises.

FLINT AND STEEL

The required materials are flint and steel, tinder, and punk. The flint can be of any fair to good grade of flint, chert, quartz or agate, or any other such rock, preferably with a beveled edge. For best results, use steel such as in the back of the closed blade of a jackknife. A belt buckle, horseshoe, etc., will suffice. The steel should be comparatively soft, since what starts the fire is the tiny particles of steel which are scraped off the metal. These fall upon the tinder and ignite it, due to friction when the steel is struck against the flint.

While some recommend a file, this is of little or no use in firemaking, because the ridges (teeth) chip away the flint, thus destroying the needed edge and also for the simple reason that files are hardened to such an extent that they do not create the particles of metal required to ignite the tinder. In short, this theory as recommended by some cannot be put into practice. To be of use, a file must first be detoothed, then softened by detempering—bringing it to an orange hue of heat in a fire.

For best results, tinder should be of charred cotton rope or cloth.

Punk can be of cattail fluff, or chunks of rotted cottonwood or willow which has been thoroughly dried out. The fleecy inner bark of cedar, cypress, or fir trees is next in order of useful materials. Birch bark has natural oils which burn even when soaked in water. Pine-heart splinters (lighters), knots, and cones afford excellent firemaking materials. Some grasses and weed umbels do very well. The nests of birds and field mice can be used. When wood is scarce, good substitutes are beaver dams, crow's nests, and packrat dens of sticks and rubbish. Dried cow chips were commonly used by the plainsmen out West.

Root wood makes the hottest fires and gives off little or no smoke. This and other materials create a gas which assists in drying out the wood ahead of the flame; this makes it burn more evenly.

Fires should be carefully controlled. One should always clear the fire site of leaves and brush to make a fire line. When leaving camp for a spell, the hot coals can be buried in the ashes in order to have fire upon returning.

To conserve matches, live coals can be carried by burying them in ashes in a tin can or vessel of pottery clay.

When making fire with the flimsy birch bark, flint-and-steel method, hold the flint horizontally in one hand while striking downward in a sharp sweeping stroke against the edge of the flint. This produces sparks which fall upon the tinder just beneath. The sparks ignite the tinder and spread. Pick up the bundle of tinder and blow gently and steadily until it bursts into a flame. Then ignite the punk, which should be kept handy.

BOW AND DRILL

There are four principal parts to the bow-drill set: the cap, the drill, the fire board, and the bow with string. (See figure 7.) The bow should not exceed seventeen inches in length and should be quite loosely strung with a one-quarter-

Survival in the Wilds / 64

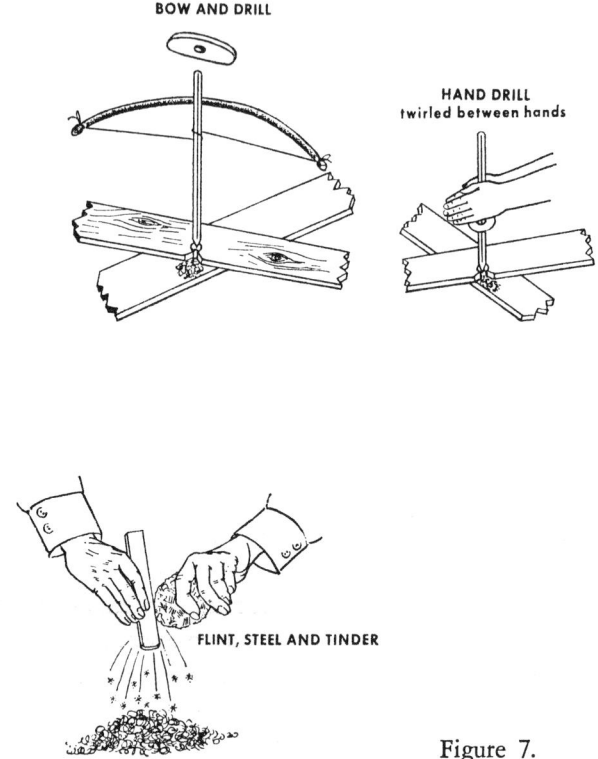

Figure 7.

inch rawhide thong or boot lace. Green silky bark of the red mulberry or a pleated string of slippery-elm bark makes a substitute string, only if freshly peeled and supple.

The cap can be a pine knot or a piece of flat rock with a slick glaze-polished surface having a small depression underneath in which to locate and seat the top of the spindle. A glass percolator top will do.

The drill should be about twelve inches long with five equal flat sides to provide traction when the string is looped tightly about it and drawn back and forth.

Firemaking / 65

The fire board or hearth can be a board or its eqivalent, three-quarters of an inch thick and any length or width. It can be a chunk of porous material, such as cactus wood. In either case, soft wood is better. Cactus, balsa, yucca, elm, or stem or root wood of cottonwood or willow are the best materials. Gummy, resinous, and coarse-grained woods such as pine, fir, walnut, oak, or sycamore are worthless.

The drill and fire board should be of the same kind of fibrous material for best results.

The right kind of wood creates a foundation of fine carbon dust, which picks up and transmits the tiny spark to the tinder when the latter is placed snugly into the notch before starting to drill.

With a board-fire pit, make a notch (an X) about three-quarters of an inch deep on the flatside of the board and start the drill point in a tiny depression made at the apex of the notch. In punklike material such as cactus, one can drill anywhere on the chunk without notching, as the pores provide the necessary oxygen and the spark is simultaneously picked up by the dust and transmitted to the wood surrounding the drill tip.

To make fire with this device, draw the bow back and forth, causing the drill to spin in the block. Start slowly with long, steady, full strokes and gradually increase the speed. When a volume of smoke begins to rise from the fire pit, you have produced a friction spark sufficient to start a fire. Lift the fire pit and add tinder. Blow gently until it bursts into flame. Fire has been made this way in six and two-thirds seconds.

Fire can be started as shown above without the use of a bow. This method requires two persons. One holds the spindle upright, supplying pressure to the cap on the spindle, and the other loops a string around the spindle with an end of a string in each hand. All one has to do is spin the spindle back and forth with the string in a sawing motion.

HAND SPINDLE

Another way to make fire by the spindle method is to omit the bow and string; merely twirl the spindle with the open palms of the hands. Since your hands tend to slide downward while spinning, make the topmost five inches of the spindle with a slightly smaller diameter than the main body of the spindle, then whittle out a wooden disk the size of a silver dollar with a center hole to fit, snugly slide it down over the upper end of the spindle and let it come to rest on the square shoulder which divides the two diameters. The edges of your hands will rest on the disk, allowing you to exert sufficient pressure to create friction. This device is more easily carried than the bow type and, of course, is operated by one person.

VINE AND FIBER

A jungle tribe builds fire by means of a simple contrivance of vine, hollow bone, and fiber. The vine fits snugly but must slip freely enough to be pushed and pulled rapidly through the hollow bone. This develops friction which ignites a spark, setting fire to cotton or other fiber when held near the end of the bone.

Take a bamboo cane and cut it directly beneath a joint. This makes a cylinder which is open at one end. Now take a piece of wood and carefully whittle out a piston to fit snugly into the cylinder. This is called a press fit. The piston should be approximately the length of the cylinder. The upper end of the piston should be smaller for easier handling. To make a fire, put some tinder or punk in the bottom of the cylinder and place the piston on top of the tinder. Now pump by rapidly pushing and pulling the piston in and out. Friction will presently ignite the tinder. Now all you have to do is to shake out the tuft of tinder and blow until the spark becomes a flame.

MAGNIFYING GLASS

Lenses of eyeglass, telescope, camera, or ordinary magnifying glass will produce fire by catching and concentrating the sun's rays to a point on a piece of tinder or punk.

GUNPOWDER

After removing the bullet from a cartridge, one can stuff cotton, cotton cloth, or tinder into the barrel of a gun and fire it into a heap of grass. This sparks the tinder so that it can be blown aflame.

SPARK PLUGS AND EXHAUST

Pull loose a spark-plug lead wire. Tie to a stick a piece of cloth saturated in gasoline, lighter fluid, or oil. Hold this in the path of the sparks arising when wire is held near the spark plug after the motor is started. This stick, rag, and gasoline method can be used as well off the exhaust pipe. One can cross a screwdriver from post to post of a hot battery and ignite a gasoline-saturated rag.

DRAWSTRING METHOD

Split a limb and wedge in a handful of tinder. Pass a string around the tinder and draw rapidly, seesaw fashion, to obtain fire by friction.

REFLECTOR

Fire can be made by concentrating the sun's rays on tinder or punk by means of copper or aluminum from an airplane or boat. Let me repeat: nature has produced certain substances and materials of low-level combustion. Some substances have a low kindling point. This is seen when such materials ignite readily by uniting them with oxygen. Subjected to a spark, they catch quickly and flames spread easily. One should know these materials, which, needless to say, will eliminate experimentation by trial and error. With such knowledge, fire can be made in all weather conditions.

One can use the reflector to start a fire with material having a higher kindling point, if they are soaked in gasoline, oil or fat. Cattail fluff is ideal.

The small fire is best for cooking and will keep a person warm by crouching near it with a blanket, coat, or parachute draped about him.

TORCHES

Useful torches can be devised in a number of ways for night traveling. A bundle of cattail spikes, that is, stems with the mature fluff saturated in cylinder oil or animal fat, makes good torches. A slab of birch bark wedged into a split stick serves as an excellent torch. Pine knots, pine cones, or splinters of the pine heart are also good. These, of course, are emergency flares.

LAMPS

The old-fashioned grease lamp is a useful item in a temporary camp. This can be made from a discarded tin can or a

Firemaking / 69

flat piece of tin formed into a dish. Some natural objects will do the job as well—shells, hollow rocks, or a hollowed-out piece of green wood.

Cotton cloth, tufts of moss, or a tab of leather are serviceable as wicks.

Eskimos cook on grease lamps. Grease is obtainable from such animals as the opossum, porcupine, woodchuck, or armadillo. Bears and seals are an excellent source of fat and oil. Animals of the deer family furnish tallow, which, when rendered, is a good substitute. Waterfowl have a good layer of fat in the fall and winter. Meat of the coconut exudes an oil when sunned. At sea one can make oil from sunned fish livers to furnish fuel for lamps and signaling.

Stoves can be made by punching ventilation holes in a large tin can. This conserves fuel and is especially good in the Arctic.

MISCELLANEOUS POINTS

To make a bed with or without a sleeping bag, one should insulate himself against the cold damp ground by spreading a thick layer of cedar, juniper, or fir boughs. Ferns or the downy fluff of the cattail is excellent insulation. In frigid zones, inside a tent or para-tepee, or in an ice or snow hut, body heat is significant, because in a confined space a certain amount accumulates.

One can build an elevated platform of forked sticks and switch poles so as to make a bed above the dampness of the ground and at the same time afford protection from snakes. This is best suited for swamp and jungle areas. Tree boughs, grass, or other materials will do for mattressing and softening the elevated bed. For making ground holes for the four-corner bedposts, simply sharpen a hardwood stick and drive it down with a club; after it is removed, put in the forked corner posts with cross poles.

With a little ingenuity, a serviceable hammock can be made. If available, a parachute could serve.

When using a sleeping bag in the Arctic, air and sun it daily to dry out body moisture or you will have a cold bed at night.

NO FIRE

At rare times conditions may make it impossible to have a fire. On one occasion, when his equipment got dunked in a stream, Daniel Boone climbed up and down a sapling all night to generate enough body heat to keep from freezing. On another occasion, when he couldn't get a fire started, he called his pack of hunting dogs to lie around him so as to keep him warm during a cold winter night.

I once had the misfortune of being stranded in severe weather and had no alternative but to do vigorous calisthenics all night long or I would have frozen to death.

7
Implementation

First of all, a jackknife is man's best friend in the woods. This knife should have several sharp blades of good steel and should be well made. Also, a good slender-bladed and sharp-pointed sheath knife adds greatly to one's security in the wilds. Another necessity is a good carborundum whetstone for honing the blades, for a dull knife is useless.

CUTTING EDGES

The most basic of all inventions is the cutting edge, from the first flint point to the knife. It is as old as man, and civilization has largely been developed by its many variations and virtues. Among other unexplored wilderness countries in the past, the United States of America was frontiered and trailblazed by the use of the knife. Take care of the knife, treat it right, and it will serve you in many ways.

A light, keen-edged hand ax or machete is very useful in out-of-the-way places.

Important points to remember: never stick a knife in a tree, in a log, or in the ground, and never lay it down. After cleaning it, always return it to the pocket or sheath when not in use.

HAND DRILL

A crude but serviceable drill can be made which is similar to the bow and drill. This requires a point to be wedged into the split end of the drill spindle. These drills were used regularly by Indians and Eskimos.

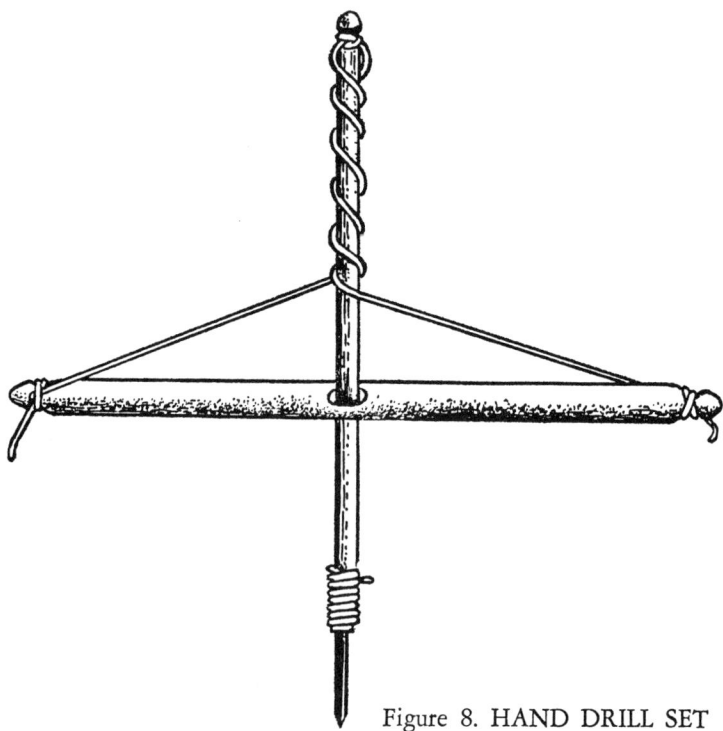

Figure 8. HAND DRILL SET

To construct this simple device, take a flat piece of wood about nine inches long, one and one-half inches wide, and three-eighths of an inch thick. Taper and notch each end. Make a hole of about five-eighths of an inch exactly in the center of the piece. Make the spindle about one-half inch in diameter with cylindrical sides and about eighteen inches long. A piece of headless nail or a slender piece of chipped flint will suffice for a bit. Place the spindle in the center hole of the crosspiece. Take a long string and mark off the middle, secure this center point around the drill with a clove hitch (one loop over the other). Tie the loose ends to the notched ends of the crosspiece. Now twist the crosspiece until the string spirals around the drill stick. Place your fingers on the crosspiece and press downward hard. This causes the string to untwist, which in turn spins the drill in the center. As this is repeated, the drill bit bores its way into the substance. This device was used by Eskimos for making holes along the sides of snow shoes for weaving the webbing. (See figure 8.)

BOW AND ARROW

Next weapon in order of importance is the bow and arrow. This is an ancient device which works silently and with deadly effect, and proved excellent for stalking. Some hunters say that it is often better than a rifle, for a well-placed shaft rarely fails to bring down the game. Many birds can be taken around rookeries (feeding and nesting grounds), and one can take meat for the pot by hiding under grapevines and berry-covered bush hovels for close shots.

Since most people have a general familiarity with the use of the bow and arrow, it needs only brief discussion. You fit the arrow nock to the string and let the tip end of the arrow rest on top of the other hand, which clutches the bow at the midsection. A little shoulder rest can be lashed to the bow for the arrow to rest upon. Face at a right angle from the quarry with feet braced, and after elevating the right arm level with shoulder, bend the bow by pulling back the string. The arrowhead should come to rest near your other hand. Aim a little high of a vital spot on the quarry to allow for trajectory. If a strong wind is blowing, aim a little to the wind side of the mark before releasing the arrow.

On occasion, when a deer takes an arrow without falling, one might have to trail your prey, especially in snow, though not too closely, and after an hour or more find it lying on the ground. When this happens, the deer will grow stiff and cannot rise. Extreme care should be exercised on approaching the wounded animal—it can be dangerous. One should shoot the deer if it attempts to arise and flee, or else the hunter may close in and club it between the eyes or cut its jugular vein. Loss of blood will weaken it till it dies. Arrows close up the wound and, unlike bullets, offer slight loss of blood by which to trail; however, internal bleeding is extensive.

In whittling the bow, flatten the face or front side of the bow and make a V shape on the backside. The V gives reinforcement to the bow. The flat face allows the bow to bend more easily.

The end notches should be tapered smaller than the midsection of the bow and on all four sides. Don't hurry in whittling and scraping out the bow. It should be flexible but strong, with sufficient springiness or cast. The lower half should be a little stronger than the upper.

For best results, use seasoned wood. Soak the wood from time to time to soften it; this makes for easier whittling.

In the American West, Indians sometimes spliced short limbs of bushes together by tapering and lashing. This was done when full lengths from trees were not available. Green or wet rawhide should be used to wrap the wood, as it tends to draw tight as it dries.

The best bow and arrow materials are listed in order of

usefulness: lemonwood, Western yew, bodock (osage orange), hickory, ash, and yucca.

If you have no knife, you can fashion a bow and arrow, spear, or other essentials by use of fire or by sharp sherds (flakes) of flintstone. Small limbs can be burnt into and scraped down to the desired size and flexibility. This is how the Indians did it. Flint can be used as a saw but it often works better as a scraper.

Modern bowstrings are made of beeswaxed linen, but in an emergency one has to improvise. First, he can cut strips from his leather belt, also cut the doubled seams from along the trousers leg and twist it for reinforcement. Multiple strands of fishing lines, which are twisted or pleated, will do. Conceivably, one might trap or snare a large animal, such as a deer, and use the skin for leather bowstrings. These should be twisted when strung. The pleated sinew tendons along a deer's back make excellent bowstrings. One can take the same kind of sinews from the tail of an opposum, muskrat, beaver, or other small animal and pleat them into a serviceable string. As a last resort, the silky bark of the red mulberry bush can serve; it is as strong as a tendon. However, it will break across the grain when dried out, so it must be carried in a moist cloth until ready to be strung and fired. When green, slippery-elm bark can be useful when pleated and strung to a bow, for small game only. Indians have been known to use their long braids of hair or the hair from horses' tails for bowstrings when all else failed. It is said that anyone can make a good bow, but the real test of ingenuity is in making the arrow.

To get straight shafts for arrows, take a good bundle of shafts in the rough and reverse the butt ends of half of them, then wrap and tie them tight from end to end and hang them up to dry. When dried, some may have slight curves which can be straightened by gently steaming over an open fire. Straighten them with the teeth or over your knee. Use a piece of sandstone rock to sand down the tiny bumps along the surface.

Arrows can be pointed or tipped by splitting the fore end, then wedging therein a thin piece of flint which has been chipped and shaped. By exerting pressure flakes can be forced from the arrowhead to make it more symmetrical and sharper. The same thing can be done with glass. Tie this on with green or wet rawhide strings or with tendons. Slippery elm or red mulberry bark will do also.

Feathers may or may not be hard to find, depending upon locality. If you are near a bird rookery or where birds frequent ponds, etc., when feeding, you should have no trouble picking up feathers. They are found under owl and hawk roosts, or where a bird has been caught by some predator. Feathers of small birds can be tied on whole; large feathers, including wing feathers, should be split and only half a feather is tied on. Tail feathers are by far the best. Glue is needed for this and can be made by cooking animals' inner hoofs or skin, or from fish skin. Now groove or nock the rearmost end to fit around the bowstring and your arrow is complete.

Jungle Indians make arrows of double length (actually short spears), as these require no feathers when aimed at close range.

The best arrow materials are cedar (Western), ash, fir, smoothed canes, palmetto stems, arrowbush, and willow sprouts. Yucca stems also can be whittled down to make arrows where better materials are scarce.

SPEARS

Spears can be used to advantage in catching turtles, frogs, fish, etc. A good spear can be improvised by lashing a sharp-pointed hunting knife to a shaft. Also, you should be able to make a crude but serviceable spear by whittling or burning a hardwood shaft to a tapered point. If whittled, it should be hardened over hot coals. A suitable flint point wedged in the split end of a shaft could not be overlooked when other means fail.

Bamboo, cut on a long slanting angle that comes to a point, makes a good spear. This can be notched on the edges to form barblike teeth with which to secure the quarry.

If one happens upon an old cabin or abandoned mine, he might find spikes or nails to use for spear points.

SLING

A sling is made of two strings of leather about two feet or longer, with a finger loop tied to the loose end of one and a knot tied at the end of the other. The strings are then tied to a sizeable leather pocket. The loop fits over the middle finger of the right hand and the knot is held between thumb and forefinger.

To operate, place a smooth solid stone in the pocket and whirl around your head once and let go of the knotted end. The sling can be quite deadly. Flung into a flock of birds or bevy of waterfowl, you will often score.

BOLA

A sometimes useful device is the bola. It is nothing more than three strings about thirty-three inches long tied together at the one end and with the loose ends each tied to a stone about the size of an egg. This device, whirled around the head once and released, wraps itself around the legs of wading birds

BOLA

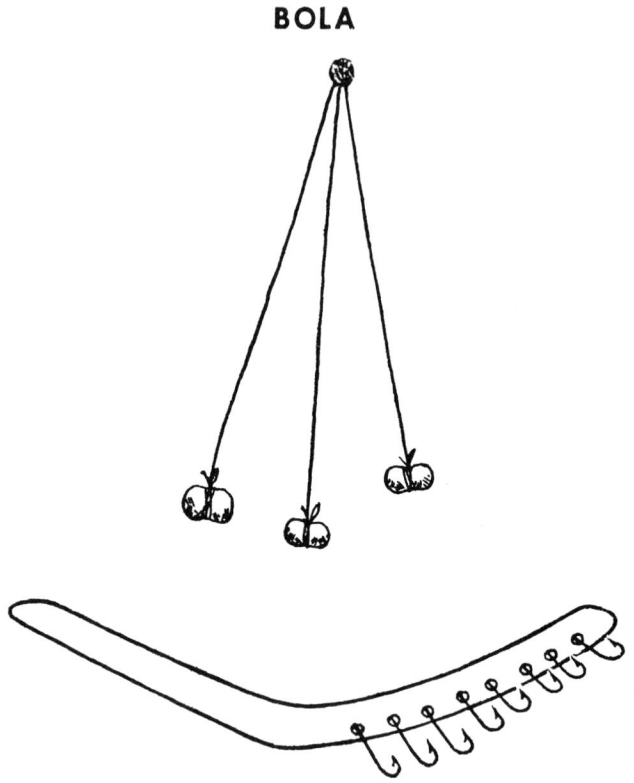

Figure 9. BOLA AND BOOMERANG WITH HOOKS

or deerlike animals, immobilizing them until a death blow can be dealt with a knife or club. (See figure 9 a & b.)

For natives in Australia a boomerang is not a bizarre weapon, but perfect design and practice make it an excellent hunting implement. With fish hooks attached it can be successfully used to bring down birds from migrating flocks.

A straight, hefty stick may be useful in taking small game, particularly porcupines, which are good to eat.

CANTEENS

Canteens are of vital importance to anyone venturing into the wilds. They can be improvised from leather, bamboo joints, birchbark, entrails and bladders of large animals—especially seals; they can also be made of pottery. Leather canteens can be made of whole skins of small animals by skinning them, starting at the hind legs and slipping the skin over the animal's head. The head and forelegs are tied off and the rear legs sewed up, except for an opening for a cane reed as a spout, which requires a bung.

Besides, one can sew up two identical pieces of leather, by punching two holes to match in each piece. These should be sewed with greased leather strings of larger diameter than the holes, so as to fill out the holes to prevent leakage. A sharp point attached to the string helps to push it through the holes. Begin lacing by starting at the mouth or corner of one side and lace around to the other side. To finish, leave an opening for a spout with bung. A carrying strap can be attached beneath the leather lacing at top sides.

Bamboo joints with the top end covered can serve by lashing leather over the opening. A string can be attached to a ringed groove near the top of the bamboo section. Canteens of birch bark can be made in exactly the same way.

Eskimos made canteens or bottles of seal entrails and animal bladders. The glazelike entrails of seals are used for making mukluks (boots), rain caps, and coats.

Indians of the Southwest made earthenware pots for storing and carrying water. (See section on pottery making later in this chapter.)

QUARTER STAFF

A quarter staff has many uses, alone or several together. This is simply a ten-foot-long pole with a pointed end. Carried by each of several in a party, they can form a tepee shelter by tying them together at the apex. Stretchers are improvised by sliding two poles down the sleeves of two coats or by folding a blanket around them. They can also serve as tripods to hang food out of the reach of pests. They are useful in vaulting or wading streams, pushing a raft or boat, or negotiating steep inclines. Shoulder blades of deer secured to them make handy shovels for moving sand, mud, snow, and the like. Neckerchiefs are easily attached to them to serve as frames for various kinds of structures.

WRITING MATERIALS

Feather quills are handy for sketching maps or taking notes. Quills are made by pointing the base of a feather and splitting it to form a pen. Ink can be made from berry juice or liquefied ashes. Slabs of birch bark or eucalyptus bark or clean sheets of leather can be used as parchment (writing paper) for map sketching or taking notes. Such crude and simple materials are of considerable help in getting oriented and on the right course.

GOGGLES

Goggles or eye slits are made simply by cutting thin slits in a two-inch band of leather and tying the ends behind the head. Eye slits can be made of wood, bone, etc. (See figure 10.) These prevent glare caused by radiation from the sun's rays reflected from water, desert, sand or snow.

For snow blindness or strong reflected light, one can mix charcoal and grease to form a smut. This is smeared on the cheekbones and face for further protection from the sun's rays.

Figure 10. ARAB TYPE HEADDRESS WITH SLIT GOGGLES

SNOWSHOES

A crude but serviceable pair of snowshoes can be fashioned from the metal rib strips of a parachute. These should be interlaced and, if possible, tied. A toe strap is tied to them a little in front of the center axis of the shoe area.

Snowshoes can be made of switch-pole frames and strings of leather or strips of parachute fabric. Any fibrous wood such as hickory, ash or elm will serve as frames. Frames should have holes drilled to match each side when bent around and tied at the rear. The holes can be drilled, as described elsewhere in this chapter, or by a sharp-pointed knife. Steam the frames before attempting to bend and tie; the form should be oval. Long, slender shoes are better for walking through brush. Strings are spaced one-half inch or less apart, each string about a quarter inch wide so as to help bear your weight. To prevent snowshoes from being snowed under or frozen to the ground when not in use, stick them upright in the snow.

BASKETRY

Carrying a basket with a strap facilitates the food gathering in whatever form. It is also useful for carrying essentials while traveling. Be sure to suspend food above the ground, out of reach of animals.

Baskets can be made of slabs of birch bark or leather, or woven of grass or fibrous tree bark. Coconut fibers lend themselves well to this purpose.

To make a basket, simply weave strands crosswise or at right angles to each other until you make the center section big enough to become the bottom, according to the size desired. The strands should lie close together. Now form the loose ends of the strands upward and continue weaving around and up the sides. Bamboo or cane reeds make excellent basketry by splitting off the outer skin in long thin strips and then weaving. To finish, the ends of the strands are woven back into the basket. Handles or straps are then inserted at the sides.

POTTERY

Pottery making is an ancient art which has survived the changes of time. For thousands of years Indians and natives of various regions relied on this method for making vessels. In modern times, clay vessels find a broad market, just as ceramics in general serve various uses. Few households are without at least one item made of clay.

Anyone forced to erect a temporary camp when lost or stranded may find it to his advantage to know the fundamentals of pottery making. Pottery clay (fire clay) is widely distributed throughout the North American continent. It is often found along cut banks and stream beds and on eroded hillsides. Deposits occur in dry areas and occasionally in the sands of Florida. Clay from ordinary dirt banks is of no use for pottery making. True pottery clay is a heavy, dense mineral earth and is often varicolored—red, pink, gray, blue, white, or brown. Clay containing foreign matter such as sand and gravel should not be used.

For clay vessels intended for cooking, powdered mollusk shells should be mixed in the clay in generous proportions. This tends to harden and temper and helps to withstand cracking when fired. To obtain the tiny flakes from oyster, mussel or clam shells, simply beat them into powder or burn them in an open fire. Indians had different methods for making clay ware but they got the same results.

Because raw clay contains air, one must mix it with pulverized shells to a somewhat fluid state and let set until the air bubbles escape. This is called "slacking" or "seasoning." When the clay is dried to a doughlike consistency, it is ready to work. Have ready a dry, circular disk of clay about the size of the bottom of the vessel desired. The new piece is rested upon it and is spun around slowly as new material is spliced in and welded to the sides.

To start the base, take egg-size pieces of clay and roll into sausage-like strips one-half inch in diameter and about six or eight inches in length. These are coiled to form the base. The base or coil should be patted out into a cake and strips added to the edge to form up the sides. These and all other parts of the coiling process are pressed together with the thumb and forefinger. This is called "welding." The coiling-splicing-welding process is continued until the desired size of the vessel has been developed. Smoothing is done in a general way while the sides are being built up; this gives it a uniform shape and surface.

The vessel should be one-quarter to three-eighths inch thick; the thinner the wall, the better. Handles can be welded on.

In firing, the piece should be turned bottom up. Have at hand a large armful of dry sticks of one to three inches in diameter to be stacked around and cover the piece. The fuel should be placed around the clay ware in tepee fashion, with none added once the fire is begun, for this would change the heat intensity. Simply let the armful of sticks burn down to ashes. Never replenish or stir the fire in any way, for this would crack the pottery. The fire alone will maintain an even heat at the right temperature. For best results, scoop out the ground for a fire pit, as this holds the heat during the firing process.

When the piece has thoroughly cooled, reheat to a red-hot color. Now take a green stick and gently lift it and submerge it in a vessel of cylinder oil, lard, or animal fat for a short time. The heat of the vessel will cause the oil to burst into flames, but no harm will be done. This operation tempers it all the more, and at the same time waterproofs the pottery. Lift it out and let the piece burn out and cool.

Water pots are best left unfired, for this leaves tiny pores in the wall through which it breathes, as evaporation will cool the water when the vessel is placed in a shady spot exposed to the wind.

You may have a more elaborately done piece with a gloss finish by glazing. This is applied to the vessel of green clay before firing. Simply take a smooth instrument or object such as a hunting-knife blade, smooth rock, or clam shell and drag and draw it; smooth it with a shiny slick surface. Usually natives ornamented their pottery by etching designs on the pieces and then painted them with ochre or red iron oxide.

Clay vessels are more easily carried by weaving a basket about them to conform to the sides and adding a carrying strap.

Earthenware vessels can be used for cooking in various ways when they are properly shaped and fire-tempered.

SOAP MAKING

In camp you can easily make up a batch of soap in a few days, as did the pioneers.

As a cleansing agent it is essential to survival, for it wards off germs that cause dysentery, skin sores, and disease in general. As a commodity it is easily obtained, since it is made of water, wood ash lye (potash), and fat.

Collect a gallon or two of wood ashes in a container and cover with water. The container can be a large tin can, several smaller vessels of clay ware, or a split hollow log with one end elevated and the other end plugged with mud or clay. Allow to set for two or three days or until the water becomes red. Now pour off the water; better still, drain it off as in the case of a hollow log. Transfer this lye water in a pot with equal proportion of fat. Fat can be obtained from such animals as the opossum, porcupine, armadillo, woodchuck, bear, or seal. Waterfowl supply rich fat. Tallow from deerlike animals makes a fair substitute for fat. Coconut oil also is good. When a fire or cooking vessel is not available, these parts can be mixed and allowed to stand for two days to get a fair soap.

Soap may be scented by stirring in some syrup of pine or fir needles, sap of sassafras root or stems, spicewood, red cedar, or flowers.

Indians obtained a fine soap by boiling the roots of the flowering yucca plant, abundant in the American West.

PREPARING ANIMAL HIDES

In curing animal hides for tanning, the animal's brains can be rubbed well into the flesh side of the hide to get a well-cured hide. If salt is plentiful, sprinkle it onto the flesh side to get equally good results. This also discourages blowflies from lay-

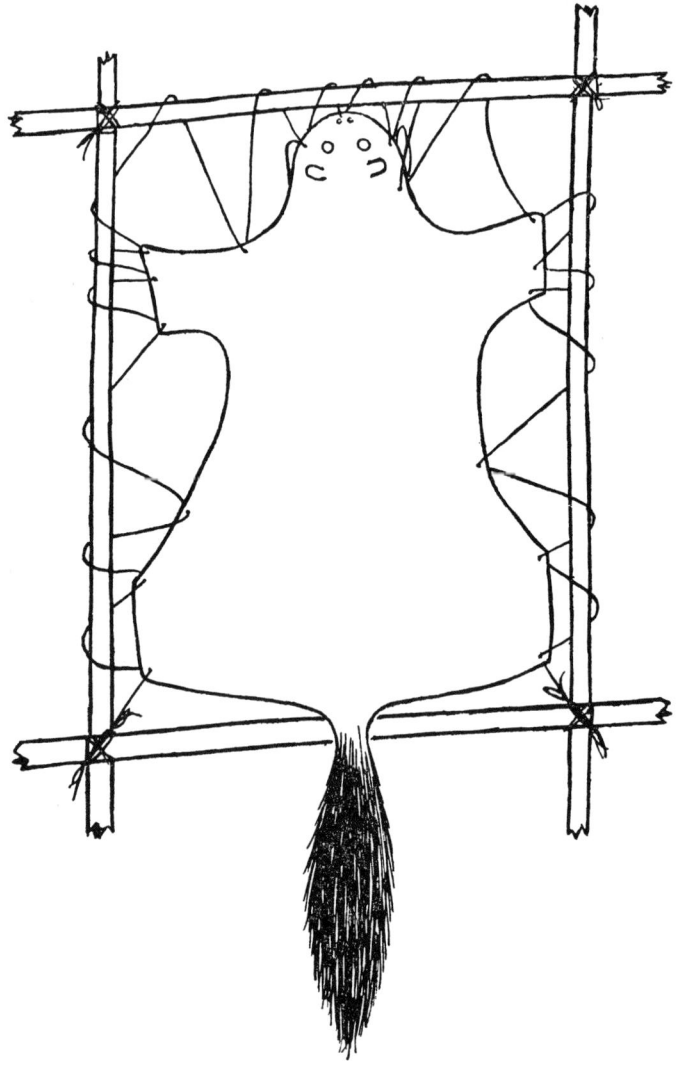

Figure 11. CURING ANIMAL HIDE ON POLE FRAME

ing their eggs, which ordinarily hatch into maggots on the fresh hide. Another good way to cure a hide is to nail it to a shelter roof or wall, flesh side out; or else stretch in within a rectangular frame of poles. This is done by using leather thongs cut from the edge of the hide and lacing them through small holes in the hide and then around the frame of poles. (See figure 11.) For best results, two persons hold the hide in place between the frame, with the head end of hide up and, then lace on opposite sides starting at the top and ending at the bottom. This should be kept in a cool, dry place where the wind will strike it broadside for a few days or until dried stiff.

TANNING

In making clothing of animal hides in a cold climate, greater warmth is obtained if the hair or fur is left on the skins. If you want to remove the hair, lay the cured hide hair side up on a smooth, hard surface and scrape the hair off, starting at the head by using the razor-sharp point of a knife or other edged instrument, such as a piece of flint or broken glass. Always work in the direction the hair is pointing.

A second method is by tying the hide securely in a creek. It should be left in the stream for several days or until the hair slips out freely when pulled with the fingers. A thin undercoat of fuzzlike hair remains after the longer hair has been pulled out. This can be removed quite easily by scraping when thoroughly dried.

A third method is by soaking it in a container of wood-ash lye (potash), as discussed in the section on soap making. The hide should be submerged in water and stirred occasionally. After thirty-six to forty-eight hours, the hair slips out freely and easily when plucked. A knife can be used to scrape it out when wet, or else with the rib bone of a deer. In this method, the hide should be soaked again and rinsed thoroughly to remove every trace of the potash residue.

The skin should be well dried preparatory to oiling, tanning, or staining. It is sometimes helpful to scuff the hide vigorously between the hands and keep this up until it is well dried, for this renders it quite supple. Otherwise it will retain its original stiffness when dry. This simple operation is of value in tanning. When the skin is thoroughly dried, oil, animal fat, or tallow should be rubbed thoroughly into the newly made leather to retain suppleness and softness and to preserve it from dampness.

Tanning may also be done by drawing the skin over a small horizontal tree limb or by placing it flat over a layer of small poles one inch in diameter and beating it with a yard-long stick, striking lengthwise and between the poles to break down the fibers. Indian squaws used to chew the skins to soften the leather.

If desired, tanned leather can be stained either by soaking it in a solution of warm water and tannic acid obtained by boiling red oak bark, or by soaking it in the verdant juices obtained by boiling the leaves and stems of various green plants. These stains produce a pleasing color and offer camouflage to the wearer who needs to blend with natural surroundings in stalking wild game.

If you must replace worn-out clothes with skins, you can get an accurate pattern by ripping out the seams of the old clothes and laying these flat on the leather material. After marking out the outline and cutting out and lacing together, the new garment will be the right size.

FISHING EQUIPMENT

The best time to catch fish is when the atmospheric pressure is rising. This occurs after a rain squall in clearing weather.

An air pressure indicator is easily made. Fill a clear jar about two-thirds full of water and put an inverted cold drink bottle in it. When pressure is bearing down, it puts a squeeze on everything including the water in the jar, causing the water to go up into the inverted bottle higher than normally occurs when placed in the jar. The water has to go somewhere, so it invariably pushes up into the bottle. When this happens, fish usually go off their feed.

A good small fish spear can be made by heating and straightening the key from a potted-meat can. Drop it into water while the metal is red hot so as to retemper it. Fishhooks also can be made of a twist key. It should be curved and pointed by hammering it out hot or cold or by sharpening it on a sandstone. The hole in the end will serve as a place to tie the line. This object also makes good needles and awls. A stone hammer can be used to pound it to a point if a hatchet is not available. If you have no pliers you can fashion a pair of crude tongs by wedging the heated key into the split end of a green stick. This prevents burning the fingers when working the piece. A belt buckle can be blacksmithed into fishhooks by the same process. These can also be made into knives for scaling and drawing out fish and game. (For improvised fishhooks, see figure 12.)

As a last resort, one might extract the long sharp heel tacks of a shoe to fashion into fishhooks. These do very well in catching pan fish if a tight line is used.

A good fish spear can be had by lashing a keen-pointed sheath knife to a pole. Flat pointed nails serve the same purpose when wedged into the split end of a long straight cane or pole. (See figure 13.)

A fish spear trap is made by splitting a long straight pole on the tapered end and driving in sharp nails from the outside toward the center and along each split half side. This resembles

Survival in the Wilds / 90

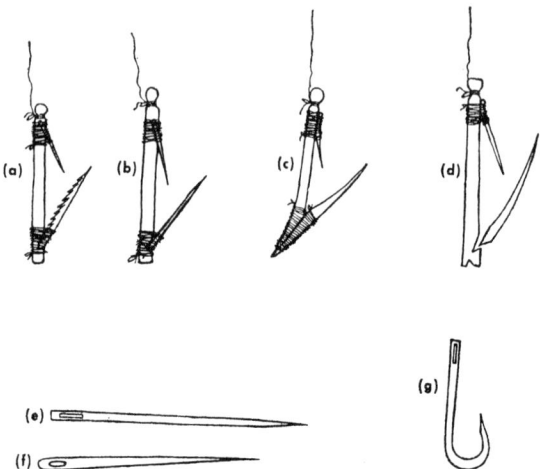

Figure 12. IMPROVISED FISHHOOKS: (a) fishhook of fish fin, (b) hook of hardwood, (c) and (d) wooden hooks, (e) needle or awl of straightened potted-meat key, (f) needle of fishfin or bone, and (g) fishhook of potted-meat key.

Figure 13. KNIFE FISH SPEAR

the jaws and teeth of a crocodile or garfish. Sharp backward notches may be used instead of nails and the split halves should be held open with a limber section of a limb. Bend it to form a U shape so it can be pushed quickly against the fish's side. When this is done, the switch limb section will be pushed out and the toothed jaws will quickly close on the fish from either side, thus securing it. A rawhide string should be lashed just behind the point where the splitting of the limb terminates.

This method is most effective when used on panfish. The spear trap is easily carried about. (See figure 14.)

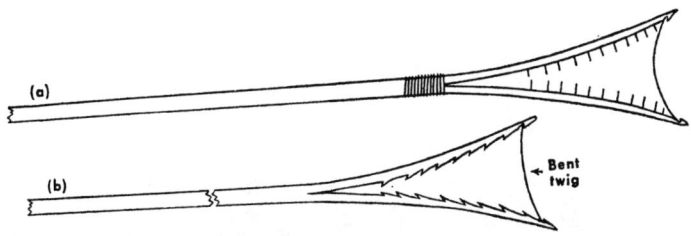

Figure 14. FISH SPEAR TRAPS

Fish fins, especially the barbed type, and bird or animal claws can be used to fashion a crude but nevertheless serviceable fish hook. Take a small piece of wood to serve as the shank of the hook and notch or bore a tiny hole at the base end and insert the fin or claw, as the case might be, and secure it. Uncured animal tendons and green-leather strings are best for tying, as they draw tight while drying. Nails sharpened to a keen point are also good. Now notch a ring around the top of the two-inch shank for tying your fish line to it. A sharp fin or stick can be tied downward and at an angle, forming a barb or whisker to keep the fish from slipping off.

Hardwoods, such as hickory, osage orange (bodock) or ironwood make adequate fishhooks when used in this manner if hardened over a fire. Fins and claws serve as needles if a tiny hole is bored into the large end. (See figure 13.)

Toggle or gorge hooks may be used on medium to large fish most effectively. This simple device can be made by whittling out a two-inch or larger piece of wood sharpened to a keen point at each end, with a groove around the center point for tying the fish line. A tab of meat or fish is skewered onto each end of the toggle to attract the fish. When the fish takes the lure, the ends of the toggle catches at right angles in the fish's throat and holds him. A dip net, if handy, should be employed in this method. (See figure 15.)

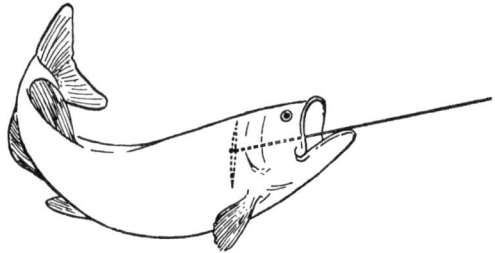

Figure 15. TOGGLE OR GORGE HOOK (skewer)

When shooting fish with bow and arrow, always aim a few inches below the fish if it is in clear, deep water. This is necessary because of refraction (bending) of light rays in the water.

A string tied to the nock of the arrow will serve to retrieve the arrow and the fish.

Fish can be attracted to a torchlight at night and may easily be speared, netted, or clubbed. One can use a sheath knife or his bare hands in taking fish drawn to the surface in this manner.

Also, fish can be grabbed barehanded in the daytime by wading in the water and feeling for the fish in likely places. Feel and look around brush and logs and undercut stones and ledges, or holes in the bank. However, beware of snakes while trying to catch fish this way.

A good way to catch fish is to improvise lures from materials that turn up in camp or in the woods. With a little ingenuity you can devise some surprisingly good lures. If ever you are lost, there is no reason why you can't put together a number of makeshift contrivances to supply your diet with fish.

A three-inch length of white or colored cloth on a hook can be dragged through the water as a fish lure. A hook wrapped in tinfoil will often succeed. Such things as the small, fuzzy feathers of birds or wisps of fur of animals make suitable flies. Hair cropped from a squirrel's tail or the fleecy inner bark of trees, such as the palm, cedar, cypress, etc., will serve the purpose. The brighter colored feathers are especially attractive to fish. The combination of red and white is excellent.

In tying the fly, wedge the eye end of the hook into the split limb of a tree to serve as a vise while you work. A limb at a convenient height should be selected. Red oxide of iron ore, or rust water, helps to stain the flies when they are soaked in it.

Solid body lures (plugs) can be whittled out to resemble a small fish which are capable of holding several hooks strategically fastened. These are attached by tying them through tiny holes burned or bored in the plug or by means of a ringed groove at the mid-section or end of the device.

When fishing through holes in ice, a shanty or tepee can be erected atop a crude sled and pulled out to the fishing spot, to protect the fisherman from cold winds. He can build a tiny fire for comfort. (See figure 16.) A tin canister of sufficient size, or rocks or clay, serve as a fire hearth. Fish caught in this manner can be piled on the ice and kept for days.

Besides artificial bait, such as flies, bugs, plugs, etc., you might use cut bait and natural bait. Cut bait may be the flesh or entrails of animals, birds, fish, or molusks. Also, small cubes of soap do very well when fishing for catfish, buffalo, or carp. Natural baits are minnows, crawfish, shrimp, insects, worms, or anything that fish ordinarily feed on.

When bait is scarce because of cold or dry weather, you are

Survival in the Wilds / 94

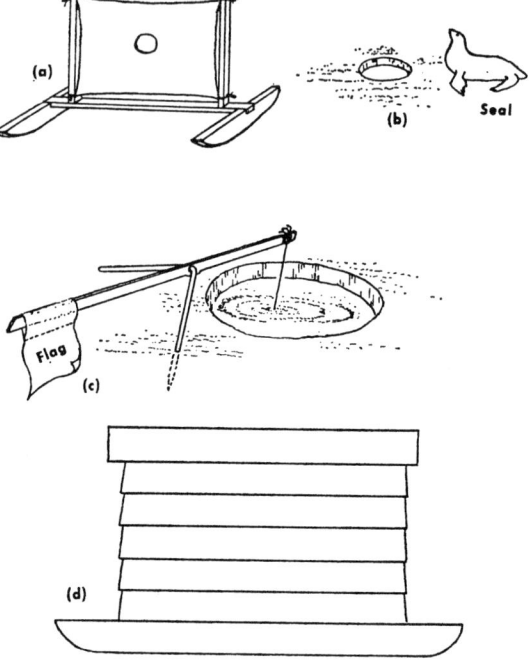

Figure 16. SLIDING BLIND FOR SHOOTING SEAL. Illustration (d) shows a floorless house on sled for fishing through hole in ice.

sure to find certain kinds of bait that will serve your needs. These can be jack-sawyers and grubs found in decayed stumps and logs. Locusts and grasshoppers afford good food for trout, bass, catfish, etc. The small worms found in nodules of the golden rod and richweed are good for taking bream, perch, and panfish in general. Excellent bream bait are the larvae of dirt-daubers and other wasps. The larvae in cocoons found in the leaves of cedar, elm, and mulberry trees are also good bait. Then there are newts, salamanders, lizards, and frogs. You can induce a bullfrog to bite a hook by dangling a red bit of cloth on a hook. Often fish can be caught by dragging one or more hooks in places where they congregate.

A quick way to get fish in abundance is to take green or mature walnuts with their husks on and, after crushing them, float them in bags in a pool of water. Loose nuts will do the job if scattered evenly. The potent juice and stain will seem to affect the fish so that they can be caught easily. If too much water runs out of the pool, it should be dammed.

8
Hunting

Throughout nature, animal and plant life are interrelated. Generally where plant life is plentiful, game is also abundant, on land and in water. Conversely, when plant life and water are scarce, animal life too is scarce. This is because animals depend on plants for food, shelter, and protection from their enemies. Plant life abounds wherever water is plentiful.

One should learn the habits and ways of animals. It shortens the gap between the hunter and the hunted, and, of course, puts more meat in the pot with less effort. Usually, technique is better than force when applied to food-getting.

In the wilderness, resourcefulness and observation are a man's best assets.

LARGE GAME

Game animals rely on sight, hearing, and smell to warn them of danger. An important advantage for the hunter is to see the game before it sees him. In the mating season it is easier to approach deer.

A good way to hunt elk is to make an imitation elk mating call, such as a whistle or bugle, to lure them.

Look for feeding places and water holes where game comes to drink. Also look for spoor (tracks) and fresh droppings, which indicate the presence of game.

Hunting / 97

In the woods one should move slowly and stop often. A motionless hunter has a decided advantage over moving game. Movement should be slow and deliberate, like that of the game being hunted, with no sudden motions.

One of the surest ways to get a good shot is to take concealment at a feeding place or water hole and lie in wait. If possible, take your station on the downwind side.

While hunting, move up wind or across wind. When sighting game, one should tack frequently, by shifting from cover to cover in order to get a good shot.

In the Far North, polar bears, which live off fish, are found in coastal regions. They never stray far from sea water. Seals can be shot on the ice or harpooned at their air holes in the ice. They can be approached by pushing a white blind on sled runners, with peephole to aim and shoot through. (See figure 16.) In the Arctic, caribou and reindeer are mammals often encountered. To make a kill, follow their tracks and stalk carefully. Stalking big game will take the utmost patience and skill. In warmer climates bears may sometimes be snow-tracked to their lair or den and shot after being smoked out. In open country, keep the sun behind you, for it is difficult to shoot facing the sun. Thus your quarry will be more readily visible. Don't silhouette yourself on a skyline, where animals will get a good look at you. Camouflage your clothes to blend with your surroundings.

Many animals are curious about strange noises or objects and are often held spellbound until you get a shot at them.

Don't follow a wounded animal too closely; give it time to bleed and weaken; otherwise it may run for miles. A wounded deer or bear will often lie down in a thicket, where it will get cold and stiffen. This is especially true of deer wounded by an arrow.

Large game can be carried on a horizontal pole placed

across the shoulders of two persons or on a travois as described earlier.

Animals, large and small, furnish many useful items from their carcasses.

Bone marrow was eaten as butter by the pioneer plainsmen, being tasty and highly nourishing. This is obtained by heating and splitting the bones.

Wild hogs (tuskers) are found in a number of Southern states, especially in Arkansas, Tennessee, Louisiana, Texas, and Florida. These are dangerous animals—never underestimate their ferocity and aggressiveness. The old boar will often charge at the slightest provocation, slashing right and left with his razor-sharp tusks. Likewise, the sow will attack if she is with young pigs.

The peccary, or javalina, is found in southwest Texas, New Mexico, Arizona, and Mexico, ranging in size from thirty-five to fifty pounds. Some hunters consider it dangerous. This animal's favorite haunt is in thickets of cactus, mesquite, and chaparral. The flesh of most wild pigs is good eating, but the peccary's scent glands must be removed before cooking.

Chitterlings can be made from the large intestines of big game. These are prepared by stripping the inner lining after turning them wrong side out by pushing a stick through them. They should be soaked in water for several days and washed clean before boiling or frying.

SMALL GAME

In most regions, small game is more plentiful than large. Small animals generally do not have the highly developed senses of the larger ones. The intelligence of small game animals ranges from the wary and alert to the slow-witted. The opossum and porcupine are examples of dull-witted animals. These can be taken with a stick or stone.

Many fur-bearing animals can be smoked out of their dens or forced out with a twist stick. This is a forked stick whittled down to a short sharp point at the forked ends The twist is effective when the forked stick is pressed against the furry side of the animal and twisted into his skin. He can now be pulled out easily.

The cottontail rabbit is to be found practically everywhere on the North American continent. Jack rabbits are usually plentiful out West. The varying hare, or snowshoe rabbit, inhabits snow country in the North, and the marsh hare, or swamp rabbit, inhabits marshy to swampy country in North Carolina, Florida, and the Mississippi Valley.

Fur of rabbits can be made into useful articles of clothing. In the north country their skins are used for stockings and mittens.

In the cold reaches of the Far North one is subject to "rabbit starvation" if he tries to live exclusively on the meat of rabbit. There, you must have plenty of fat in your diet to supply the calories necessary to contend with the bitter cold. Fat also helps generate body heat.

A person can survive off his fat and muscle for weeks, but eventually he must have fat in his diet or he will starve. During the days of beaver trappers, the tail of the beaver was much coveted for its tenderness and delicate flavor. However, other parts of the animal are edible.

In the southern United States many people eat muskrat and consider it a delicacy. These are canned and sold as "marsh hare." The muskrat is a very clean animal; its food is mainly cattail and flag roots and tender plants in general. In some small animals certain glands must be removed, as they impart an undesirable taste to the meat.

In the Arctic, the lemming is good emergency food if provisions are scant. These can be killed with a stick or stone or dug out of the snow. Rodents, plentiful in the West, should not be passed up; they are a rich source of food.

Reptiles offer an available food supply if one is starving. Lizards too are considered a delicacy by the desert Indians.

If poisonous snakes are to be eaten, make sure the reptile has not bitten itself, which rattlesnakes sometimes do when molested.

BIRDS

Birds often congregate in great numbers and can be taken by shooting, trapping, or snaring. Sometimes one can throw a stick or stone and score a kill. They can be found along sea shores, islands, and marshes, and on cliffs in the Arctic. These places are inhabited by birds the year round. Crows and grackles migrate to a warm climate during the fall of the year.

Eggs are good in all stages; even the unhatched chick is of value as food.

Fledglings are an easily obtainable source of food wherever they are found and can be hunted to advantage around nesting and roosting havens, or rookeries.

The heads of birds as well as those of small animals are edible; brains are quite good and nourishing.

Certain birds, also squirrels, store up acorns and nuts in hollows of trees in the fall of the year; these can be exploited after the snow has covered the ground and the storage places are discovered by tracking.

Birds at sea sometimes land and rest on boats and rafts and are easily caught. Simply trail a hook and line behind a life raft, baited with a shiny or colored object or fish entrails, and birds following behind will dive for the bait. In doing so, the hook gets caught in the bird's gullet.

Often where land birds congregate, this trick will supply you with as many birds as you need. Entrails, chunks of fish or meat, and even berries on the hook are all effective bait.

One can occasionally pick up a free meal by scaring a hawk or predacious bird away from its kill. The bird will almost always drop the prey, to return to the feast later.

AQUATIC ANIMALS AND SHELLFISH

On survival status, fish, including shellfish, can make up a large portion of the daily food quota. Streams and other bodies of water are reservoirs of food. Generally, animal life is more abundant in water than on land, as it is concentrated in a more limited area and often is more easily obtained.

The chance of survival beside a body of water is excellent, especially along the sea shore where there are countless fish, crustaceans, turtles, and birds. Aquatic life is practically inexhaustible. Most saltwater fish can be eaten raw. Usually, early morning, evening and nighttime are the best times to fish, no matter what method is employed.

Sea weeds found in the water and along the beach are rich in food value.

One can chop or burn down a tree and let it fall into a body of water to make a place for access to deeper water and more fish. Fish congregate in schools around tree tops. One can put out set hooks and be certain to make a catch.

After catching your first fish, cut it open to see what the fish has been feeding on, then try to use similar bait.

Seafood should be eaten soon after it is caught; it soon spoils in warm climate.

Cooked rough fish, such as gar, carp, and mudfish, should be eaten hot, or boiled and made into patties for frying.

Fish, shrimp, and crabs inhabit masses of seaweeds. By using a grappling hook on a line one can drag it behind a boat and collect seaweed which, when shaken well, will give you crustaceans enough for a good meal.

Eskimos eat fingerling fish and minnows on the spot, uncooked. And don't throw away fish heads; they make fine chowder or stew.

CRUSTACEANS

Crustaceans are delectable food, best when baked, but usually are dropped live into boiling water. Little effort is required in catching them, and there are several ways of doing so. The shellfish are usually taken in a sieve or dip net, but they are also speared or caught barehanded when no other means are handy.

Crayfish can be collected by turning over stones in a creek. Shrimp inhabit alkaline water, both fresh and salt. One can easily catch crawfish, lobsters, or crabs by dangling a piece of meat or fish on a line near the bottom and slowly drawing it up from time to time. A dip net should be used to catch them, as they fall off the bait when it is surfaced.

Mollusks can be spotted in lakes and streams, and mussels and clams can be picked up at low tide or in the ocean shallows of inlets and bays. Mussels are mostly to be found in lakes and streams, but they also inhabit rivers where the sea tide flows. Leave them in the sun until they open, or else insert a knife at either end of the shell to cut the tendons. A molusk that doesn't close when handled is either dying or dead and is probably unfit to eat.

Oysters are found along all of the seashores of the United

States and Canada and grow in barlike masses in shallow water. These groupings or bars can be pried loose in large chunks and shelled somewhere out of the sunlight. In hot weather they will keep unspoiled for two or three days if water is dashed on them every few hours. Oysters are good raw, steam-baked, fried, or boiled.

Be careful not to eat contaminated oysters—they can cause ptomaine. Oysters taken where sewage is drained into their area are infested with microscopic worms transmitted from excreta. Steer clear of places that are likely to be used for sewage disposal.

Coquina shells, which are tiny and varicolored, can be scratched or dug out of the sand as each wave recedes. They occur in hundreds within a two- or three-foot area just under the sand.

Conchs and whelks found in the bays and in the sea proper provide a rich, red soup, and the meat is delicious.

Gars can be baked in their hulls, if preferred, when the entrails have been drawn. Otherwise, when skinning off their armorlike hull it can be split along the back or belly, or it can be removed in a spiral manner. Gars' meat might be compared to that of catfish, and they are clean, as they eat only live fish, whereas catfish are scavengers.

Mudfish, also called bowfins, grindle, or scaledling are carryovers from prehistoric times and can live for extended periods in mud, being equipped with lungs as well as gills. Such fish can easily be caught by hand as a water hole dries.

TURTLES AND OTHER FOOD

Turtles can be taken in traps or by hook and line. They are often seen migrating from one water hole to another.

Indian children and squaws were known to scout the area

surrounding camp for the box tortoise as a food supplement. These amphibians are easily caught.

Gopher turtles, which grow to considerable size in Florida, may be seen throughout most of the year. During the winter, they tunnel into the sand dunes and hibernate. Rattlesnakes often share the holes with them. One can dig out a gopher turtle by taking a long sharp stick and trace out his tunnel by punching into the sand.

Turtle eggs in the spring are edible raw or cooked. Roasting is the best way to prepare them, as they remain rubbery even when boiled.

Frogs can be caught on hook and line by inducing them to strike at a bare hook or by using a small piece of red cloth or worm or bug on the hook. Frogs can also be caught by bow and arrow, by gigging, or you can rap-switch small ones on the ground. If you have never eaten frogs' legs, you are missing something; they are delicious.

Grasshoppers, earthworms, and snails are edible. These can be roasted in or out of clay balls or can be made into a soup. You might not relish them, but they are a staple in certain parts of the world, and they will keep you alive in case of extremity.

9
Plants

Plants of all kinds are a valuable source of food. They contain many vital ingredients necessary for survival. One can eat all sorts of roots, bark, flowers, or fruit and subsist indefinitely.

A person can live off his own fat and muscle tissue for weeks, but after a time he must have the benefits derived from vegetation, or disease will set in. Scurvy, for example, is avoided or cured by drinking tea made by steeping pine needles in water. Spruce bark serves equally well. Any fruit juice serves this purpose.

Honey comes originally from plants and helps to prevent fatigue and disease, furnishing quick energy when one is exhausted. Mountain climbers make use of it before undertaking a difficult ascent.

Wild honey can be found in rock crevasses on the desert in the western United States where trees with hollows do not exist. If you haven't an ax, you can burn down a bee tree and then burn out the honeycomb. If available, mosquito netting should be used over exposed parts, especially the face when attempting to invade a wild bee hive. Cold weather immobilizes the bees.

MUSHROOMS

While there are many edible mushrooms, especially in tem-

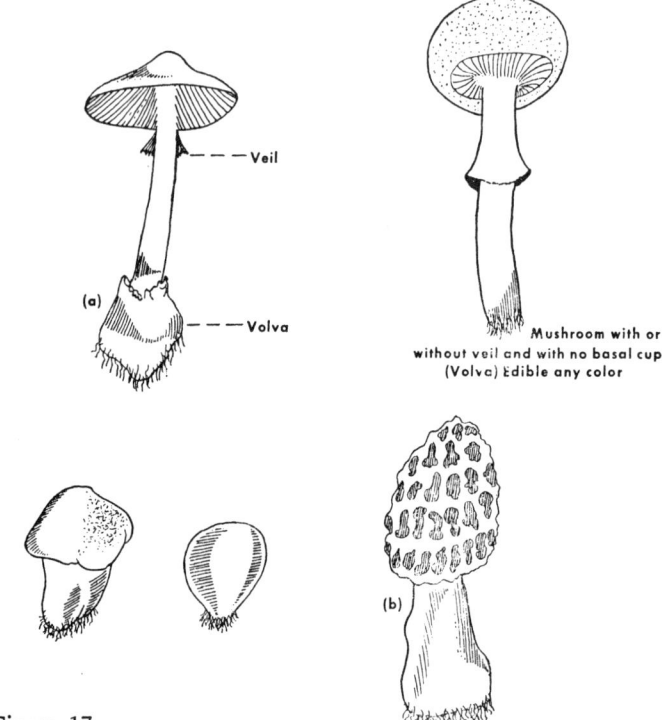

Figure 17.

perate regions, no species should be eaten unless one is sure of its identity, because some of them are deadly poisonous. (See figure 17.)

Squirrels eat all kinds of mushrooms, but those which the squirrels are seen eating are not always safe for human consumption.

The most widespread among the poisonous mushrooms are the amanitas, which have a frill or ring or veil around the upper part of the stem, a sac (volva) at the bottom, and a white spore deposit which drops out of the gills. Do not eat any mushroom which these three characteristics. No poisonous mushrooms have been reported in northwest Canada. The only poisonous mushroom in Alaska is the amanita.

Puffballs, sometimes called "devil's snuffbox," are more or less globular bodies that develop their spores inside and have a solid white interior when young. Many of these are edible when fresh. Mushrooms called puffballs grow to the size of small pumpkins and lend a banquet touch when fried with venison or trout.

Mushrooms may be stewed or rolled up in clay and baked. They may be dried and kept for later use.

Morels are easily recognized and all are edible. These have a crinkly or pitted top as if shriveled.

"Indian bread," called tuckahoe, is an edible subterranean fungus found in mountainous areas. This grows in a ball shape and is also a term for the rootstock of certain plants.

The nutlike seed pods of the poisonous buckeye can be eaten when prepared and rendered safe, as did the Indians. These should be boiled four or five times to eliminate the poison. Each boiling requires a change to fresh water. Acorns may also be freed of the tannic acid by boiling thoroughly. All these can be dried well and pulverized into a flourlike powder for breadstuffs. Red-oak acorns have too much tannin to be of use as food.

Besides buckeyes and acorns there are beechnuts, hazelnuts, walnuts (black and white), piñon nuts, pecan, and coconut, which are excellent food.

Some plants yield fruit in the form of beans which are similar to lentils. These are the pawpaw, locust, mesquite, jojoba, mescal bean, and yellow paloverde.

The locust bean has a honeylike substance which can be scraped out with a knife and eaten like jam or fruit butter. This is highly nourishing because of its sugar content.

There are a number of succulent fruits of a fleshy nature which are good to eat and in most cases pleasing to the taste. These supplement a meal and provide sugar energy. In some cases, the seeds are inedible, such as the may apple, maypop, persimmon, wild plum, and wild lime. Also there are prickly-pear cactus, which bear edible fruit, similar to the fruit of the giant saguara cactus plant. These are gathered when ripe in July by splicing poles together and getting down those within reach.

FRUITS

One may subsist on berries for an extended period of time. Among them are the wild strawberry, dewberry, raspberry, mulberry, huckleberry, service berry, sparkle berry, cranberry, salmonberry, sageberry, buckbrush berry, and red and black haws.

Wild currants, grapes, muscadines, and choke cherries are plentiful in many areas. All of these ripen from May to November, according to kind and locality.

Human beings and many animals depend upon cereal grain for food. All grass seeds are edible and are best when roasted or made into a gruel.

Pinole are edible seeds of various American plants, prepared for later use by roasting.

A few wild grains are wild rice, millet, seeds of lilypads in northwestern America, and seeds of the bamboo which bear at long intervals. Turtle grass along salt marshes and seashores bears edible seeds.

These grains can be crushed or ground into flour as the Indian did by pounding them into a fine powder in a hollowed stone—the mortar-and-pestle principle. This is called a metate. The method is still used in desert areas.

Grain can be separated from the chaff by winnowing or pouring it into a cloth, blanket, or deerskin while a stiff breeze is blowing.

BEVERAGES FROM PLANTS

Some plants which have little food value can be used for making stimulating and refreshing beverages. The roots and bark of red sassafras, stems of the spicebush, bark of black birch, red sumac berries, blackberry leaves, leaves of wintergreen Labrador tea bush, and spruce bark all can be used in making tea. Dandelion leaves and leaves of chickory produce palatable drinks when steeped or boiled. Acorns furnish a kind of tea, boiled after they are roasted.

BARK AS FOOD

The tender inner bark of numerous trees is a source of food which should not be overlooked, and can be eaten raw or cooked. In famine areas, people make bread from the inner bark of trees. Brown bark contains too much tannin. Among trees whose bark is used for food are the poplars (including the cottonwood and aspen) birches, and willow, the inner bark of a few species of pines, such as the lodgepole or shorepine of western North America.

The outer bark is scraped or stripped off and the inner bark is eaten raw, dried, or cooked. It is a good ingredient in hunter's stew. This bark is more easily obtained in the spring of the year, and can be dried for later use.

The leaves, stems, buds, bulbs, roots, and blossoms of plants are edible and make good food stretchers. The stems of some plants are excellent, furnishing starch, sugar, oils, and greens. The blossoms are rich in vitamins.

Most edible roots are of a fleshy nature. Examples are the wild potato and wild yam. The arrowhead plant has an edible tuber; also Solomon's-seal, which is like parsnip. The arrowroot has carrot- or potato-like roots and is not good eaten raw.

The wild-onion bulb and blades may be eaten as a relish or may be cooked into a stew. Cattail bulbs and roots are good raw, roasted, or boiled, and can be dried for keeping. This plant will be discussed under special plants of value.

The camass has a fine edible bulb which was relied upon for food by the Lewis and Clark expedition. Indians assisted them in getting the bulbs, which are much like onions and have flowers with long slender petals, purple with a blue streak at the center. Other varieties of this species are poisonous, such as the death camass, deadly to man and beast. Those with purple petals and blue streak down the center are safe to eat.

Wild tender ferns have edible roots and furnish greens, as does dandelion, purslane, narrow dock, lambs'-quarters, sheep sorrel, and pokeweed. Plantain shoreweed may be eaten as lettuce. Wild lettuce is found in swamps of tropical and semitropical areas, and what is used is only the part not exposed to the water. Thistle root is good raw, roasted, or boiled. An edible wild carrot is to be found in the North. The nut grass and water chestnut have edible tubers; also the bulrush, which has an edible stem base.

STARVATION

If no food is to be had for days, it is important to remember you can survive a long time by drinking a solution of water, sugar, and salt in moderate proportions. These or their substitutes are to be found in nature throughout many areas. Food bulk with little or no food value can alleviate hunger pangs while you are on a liquid diet.

SPECIAL PLANTS AND FIBERS

Certain plants were vital to the Indians. Consider the lowly cattail. From it one can gather pollen from the spikes in the spring. This is rich in vitamin content. (See figure 6.) The fluff is useful for fire making in various ways, and also furnishes fuel for warmth and cooking purposes. When burned, it generates intense heat, yet produces little or no smoke. The fluff can be used for bandages in dressing cuts and wounds—in fact, it was used for this purpose during World War I. It keeps out harmful germs and is easily flushed off the wound with warm water. An excellent bedding is another of its virtues, if a quantity of the fluffy substance is put on the ground for insulation and warmth, as good as any down.

A good life preserver can be made by stuffing it in a bag, which is improvised by tying trouser legs into knots and knotting the ends. One can also make basket-like bags woven from grass or sedge, or by using fibrous bark from certain trees, as will be described presently. This buoyant cattail fluff, found the country over, was used a great deal during World War II and proved even better than kapok. One can make a crude but serviceable boatlike flotilla by constructing a frame of light willow poles in the shape of a boat and fastening a series of fluff-filled bags around it.

An excellent torch can be made from the fluffed spike, using the stalk as a handle. The spike is soaked in cylinder oil or in oil from rendered animal fat.

During the spring, water is stored in the pithy stalk: this is one of nature's ways of purifying water amid muck and contamination. To extract the water, simply peel off the outer skin and chew the pith.

Boat paddles can be improvised by combining the stems,

half the bases reversed. Tied together, the bundle should just fit the hand for easy paddling.

The long slender blades can be woven into mats, stacked one on top of another on a frame of poles, to form a windbreak or sun shelter. They can also be made into baskets for keeping fish or, to gather wild herbs, nuts, or fruit.

Bulbs, as already mentioned, can be eaten raw or cooked. To cook, put a bunch of bulbs on the hot coals of an open fire with their shucks for twenty minutes; they are then ready to eat, tasting much like steamed cabbage. Season with salt, pepper and butter. They also taste good when boiled or baked in clay.

Roots can be eaten raw or cooked; they make a starchy, potato-like paste.

YUCCA

Yucca, a valuable plant, is found throughout most of the Western states and Mexico. (See figure 18.) Stems make a

Figure 18.
FLOWERING
YUCCA

fair substitute for bow material when nothing better is available. The smaller stems will suit as arrows.

The leaves can be soaked in hot water then pounded with a club to obtain ropelike fibers that can be used for ropes, lashings, bow strings, fish lines, baskets, and sandals.

In a museum adjacent to the Capitol Building in Denver, Colorado, a shaving brush of yucca fiber is on exhibit; it was used by Kit Carson during his journeys into the Rockies.

Desert Indians used the fibers for making ropes, baskets, sandals, and even clothing.

A fine ready-made soap is made from the juices of the yucca roots.

PALMS

Palms are found along the southern coastline of the Gulf states, in certain desert oases and in parts of Mexico. This tree is sometimes found inland in swampy areas of the deep South, particularly in Florida.

When cooked, the buds are excellent eating, best when prepared with meat or fish. They also can be eaten raw—called "millionaire's salad." They contain a quantity of sap and is a good water substitute. To get the bud, you cut away the "boots" at the base of the leaves and eat the tender base of the bud.

Leaf fans have been and still are in use as roof shingles by Indians and whites alike. The leaf stems make good arrow shafts when cut out to size in the green state and allowed to season properly. The leaf fibers can be pleated into ropes or fishing lines. Leaf fans serve as plates on which to put food; also, they can be used to cover freshly caught fish or game to keep off insects, and serve as fans in hot weather. Along with Spanish moss, they supply natives with bedding materials, as protection from cold or damp ground.

Fiber matting can be fashioned into rope, baskets, sandals, bedding material, fish nets, and can be used as wicks for grease lamps.

One can burn the trunks of palm trees and, by boiling down, obtain salt from the ash.

One can eat the jelly-like meat of the green coconut, which, contrary to popular opinion, is better than the meat of the ripe nut. Sprouting nuts are good to eat, and the ripe nut contains water as well as nourishing food. Traveling over land or sea, a supply of coconuts are sufficient for an extended journey.

Oil is collected from the meat (copra) of the ripe nut by heating or sunning, and is made into balm, lamp fuel, or soap. Palms also have clusters of seeds that are edible and nourishing.

TESTING PLANTS FOR TOXICITY

If you are not sure if a plant or parts of it are safe to eat, try a teaspoonful and wait eight hours. If no harmful effects, eat a handful and again wait eight hours. You can then venture a full meal. This is how the Indians tested unknown foodstuffs, and is the only safe method of discovering whether it contains any poisonous properties.

10
Cooking and Preserving Food

Cooking renders most foods palatable and digestible, destroys bacteria, toxins, and harmful animal and plant products. Food should be cooked whenever possible. The best cooking is done over a bed of coals rather than over flames. Build up a good-sized pile of wood on a fire and let it burn down to a bed of coals. Feed it small green wood occasionally to maintain heat. Small fires are best.

Boiling requires a container. Since tough meat has to be cooked a long time, it is often wise to boil it first, then roast, fry, or bake it. Boiling is a good method in cold climates, especially when you want to save the juices. At high altitudes, food must cook longer than at low altitudes, because of the reduced oxygen where the air is thin. Don't try to boil food above twelve thousand feet; it would require too much time and too much fuel.

Water in a chopped-out hole in a log or clay pit can be heated by dropping hot stones into it. A deerskin or strip of canvas can serve in the same way; place it in a depression in the ground and use it to heat water and boil food by dropping in hot stones. The stones should be changed from time to time. A serviceable pair of tongs for handling the stones can be made of a green tree limb, such as hickory, ash, or elm, by bending it double, with a spoon-shaped cavity fashioned at the ends.

Stones for heating should not be taken from stream beds; they contain water and will explode when heated. Also, limestone should not be used because the lime content, when heated, will explode to a certain degree.

A green coconut shell with the stem end cut or a length of a green bamboo joint can be used to boil food. (See figure 19.)

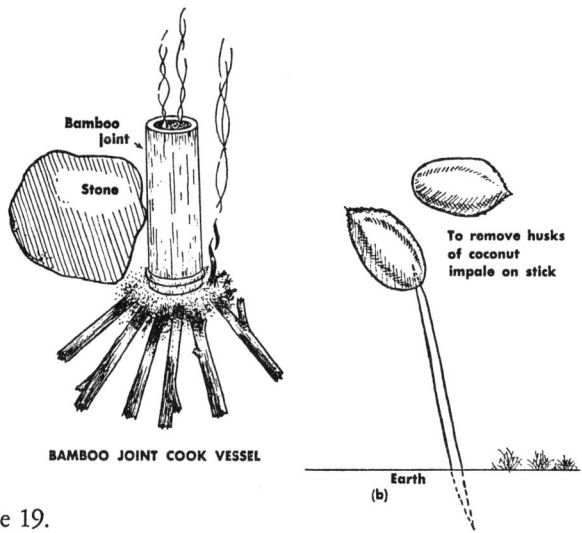

Figure 19.

The bamboo joint should have a green leaf tier around the open (top) end of the joint section to hold in the steam. Keep the joint standing upright in the fire by leaning it against a log or rock. This will not burn through before the stew is fully cooked. With tough meat, you may have to change over to another joint, as it will require more cooking time, thus more burning of the bamboo.

Cooking and Preserving Food / 117

While cooking, keep a water container at hand. A long piece of bamboo is adequate; punch the joint partitions out, all except the bottom one, or use several single joint sections for water.

Water can be boiled in a birch-bark trough or container, for the fire will not burn below the water line. Keep the top edge moistened. Tea can be made in such vessels. Inverted turtle shells will also serve. In such containers the meat, fish, or herbs should be cut very fine to facilitate the cooking process.

Plates may be substituted with large green leaves such as palm and the like. Birch bark in slabs serves well in this respect.

Natives of the sea islands have been known to use turtle shells for food vessels and clam shells for spoons.

When cooking above ground, pots and pans are put across logs or stones or suspended over the fire by means of a crown pole, the ends of which rest in forked posts. Flat stones are best for supporting cooking vessels; they should be somewhat higher than the bed of coals.

Meat, herbs, and fish can be cooked on a sharp, green, hardwood stick. When fish is cooked on a sharpened stick, the point should be thrust through the fish's mouth and through the body to its tail. A racket-like affair can be made for grilling fish by taking a forked green stick with a spike stem in the center and weaving cross sticks through the tines. (See figure 20.) Fish can be rolled up in mud and baked. Another good way to broil fish is to suspend a pole between forked posts and hook a limb through the fish's gills, hanging it vertically from the horizontal pole. Fish, baked or broiled, should have the skin and scales left on to prevent the flaky flesh from separating.

Twist bread can be baked on a freshly peeled green stick by twisting a long piece of dough around it. Each end should be baked first to prevent unraveling. (See figure 21.)

Survival in the Wilds / 118

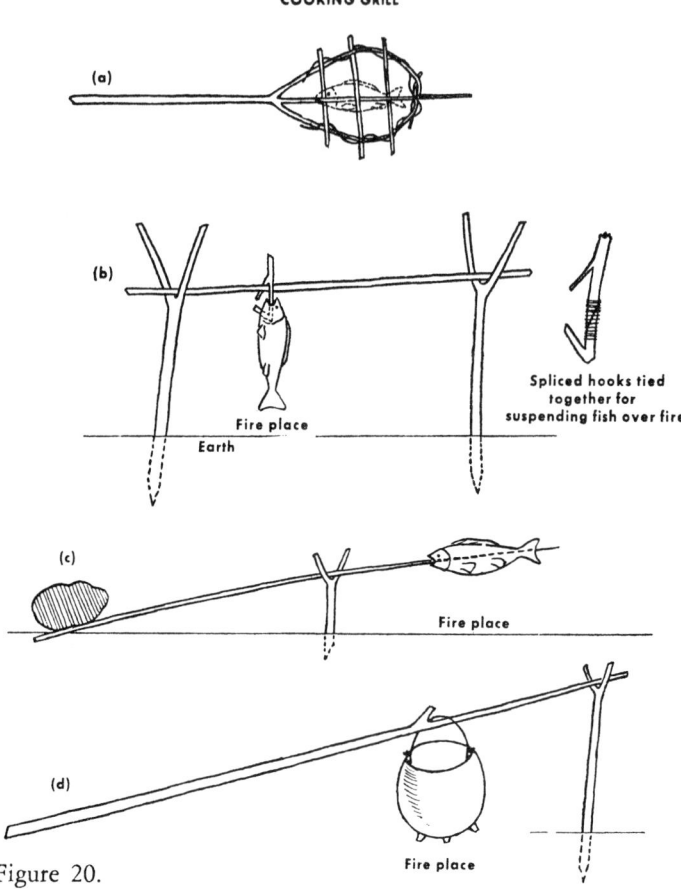

Figure 20.

Many meats, fish, vegetables, herbs, and fruits can be cooked by placing them on the open fire or by rolling them up in balls of stiff clay.

Fish, meat, vegetables, and bread can be prepared by slicing them extra thin and placing them on a tilted reflector of split logs of small-log size. (See figure 22.) Hot flat stones are

Cooking and Preserving Food / 119

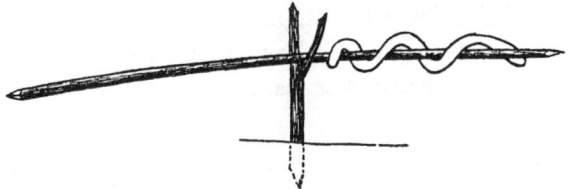

Figure 21. TWIST BAKED BREAD

used in a similar way, tilted or flat. Such fare can be cooked on sun-heated flat stones in hot desert areas by changing them from one stone to another as the stones cool. Food can also be cooked, sliced thin, by placing on sun-heated metal wings of airplanes or metal boats. Aluminum, copper, and iron sheets absorb and hold heat well.

Figure 22. LOG HEAT REFLECTOR

Sheets of aluminum foil ought to be in any survival kit, for nearly any kind of food can be wrapped up in it and cooked by burying it in a bed of hot coals.

BREAD OVEN

Indians of the Southwest and Mexico use ovens of adobe for baking bread. These unique devices are the shape of an Eskimo igloo. All one has to do is to build a hot fire in the oven and, when thoroughly heated, rake out the coals and put in the bread. A clay block is used to fit the opening snugly so as to trap the heat for baking. A ventilation hole may be made in the top or rear.

TURTLES

With the soft-shelled turtles, shell and all can be boiled until the meat separates. Fat is removed, as it imparts a rank flavor to the meat. If you don't have an ax to cut loose the carapace under the belly, burn each side of it at the edge of an open fire and whack it loose with a club. It should now be dressed out for cooking. After stewing, the meat can be made into patties and fried.

CRUSTACEANS

Crabs, prawns, crayfish, and shrimp can be roasted, boiled, or baked. The best way is to drop them in boiling water. They cook quickly, and should be cooked soon after catching because they soon spoil.

All shellfish can be steamed, boiled, or baked in the shell. Oysters, of course, are good raw. Mollusks make excellent stews in combination with tubers and greens.

Cooking and Preserving Food / 121

The fleshy, tender, inner bark of certain trees (poplar, birch, willow) can be added to most stews.

MISCELLANEOUS COOKING

Locusts (grasshoppers) and snails can be roasted, baked, boiled, or fried, but are best disguised in stews with other foods.

Eggs can be boiled and carried for days in moderately cool weather. They can be poached in any kind of makeshift container, such as a coconut shell or bamboo joint. They can be fried on any grate of metal or on a flat rock, or even eaten raw.

Fresh papaya leaves in the tropics contain papain which renders meat soft and tender in a short time. It is especially useful when meat is to be eaten raw or partly cooked.

The citric acid in limes, lemons, or similar fruits can be used for pickling meat and fish. Dilute two parts of citric juice with one part of sea water, add meat, and allow to stand for half a day or more. The citric acid will cook the flesh. The meat or fish should be chopped or sliced extra thin.

As a last resort for cooking, one can make a steam pit. Dig a hole in the ground about two feet wide and two and a half feet deep. Line the hole with hot stones and, after putting in a layer of damp seaweed or green leaves, set the meat, herbs, fish, or clams or a combination of them. Slice the meat thin and place it on top to receive most of the heat. Then put in more green leaves and seal the hole with a large slab of readied clay. Now punch a hole in the center of the mud in a funnel shape. Pour in two quarts of water and close up the hole. The entire operation should be done quickly; have everything ready at hand. To hold the pressure, set stones on the pit cover to weight it down. You may now go hunting and return after a couple of hours to a tasty meal.

HOBO STOVE

One can use a small can partly filled with water, the rest with gasoline, and improvise a good serviceable stove for heating and cooking. The floating gasoline, of course, is the burning fuel.

SUGAR AND SALT

Sugar is essential for energy and can be obtained by boiling sap of the sugar maple tree. Natural sugars are found in wild honey and wild fruit.

Salt is a necessary part of the human diet. It is obtained by boiling sea water, water from a salt spring, or by boiling ashes from hickory or palm trees. The residue, when boiled, leaves a black-looking salt.

PRESERVATION OF FOOD

In the far reaches of wild country, it is well to prepare and carry an extra supply of food by preserving it. There may be many days when an emergency puts you in dire need of subsistence. When this happens, you will be grateful for any form of nourishment that you have prepared for such an event. The emergency could arise from a siege of foul weather, such as a blizzard, or during days of heavy rainfall when it is difficult if not impossible to find food. There might be a time when you do not chance upon food of any kind.

Food, both plant and animal, can be preserved by crude but effective means, and it will keep indefinitely. The methods have been tried and proved by Indians and settlers, and can be of great value to anyone who has to spend a long time in some isolated part of the world.

JERKY

Jerky can be made of any large or small animal or fish. Slice long thin pieces of meat and hang them on poles exposed to the dry wind and the sun. Jerky is best made in the American West. The drying process reduces the moisture content to a minimum; what takes place, in other words, is dehydration.

Meat and fish alike can be kept by freezing.

SMOKED MEAT AND FISH

To smoke meat, cut long thin pieces and hang it on pole racks within an enclosure. This may be any shelter, usually in tepee fashion, which has been made of poles and sod or of large slabs or bark.

For best results as to taste, use turnings of green hickory; next best ash or oak. Always use a nonresinous hardwood. Smoke the meat continuously for twelve hours or until the meat ceases to curl. It is then ready to store and use. Do not place cured meat in a container for long without ventilation unless the weather is cold. Baskets do very well. Otherwise it will mold and spoil.

Fish can be smoked the same way. Split up one side from the tail to head and then up the other side; now remove the entire backbone section. This leaves the head joined to the two side fillets, forming a hairpin shape which can easily be hung on horizontal pole racks for curing. The raw backbone section can be made into chowder when prepared for smoking; the heads also can be used similarly.

Blow flies are not attracted by jerky or smoked meat. Meat so cured keeps indefinitely in any weather. However, smoked fish does not keep for more than a few weeks, except in cool weather.

Wild herbs and fruit can be dried the same way (dehydrated).

PEMMICAN

This was a favorite method of Indians because it afforded a highly nutritious food which kept them through long winters or during summer travels. Pemmican is made simply by drying small bits of meat and berries or other wild fruit and mixing them after pouring on a generous quantity of animal fat or tallow. During the winter this can be hung up in baskets or leather bags.

PINOLE

Pinole is roasted grain that keeps in all weather and is used to make a coffee or tea substitute which provides nourishment.

SALTING

Fresh meat or herbs can be preserved by pickling in heavy brine. Pemmican or other foods can be kept encased in cleaned and dried animal intestines.

BLANCHING

Meat will keep for a considerable time by blanching (partly boiling) it. Boil the meat until it turns white, then drop it into containers of hot fat or tallow.

11
Shelter

Since man's beginning, shelter has been an important link in the survival chain. When beset by adverse circumstances, such as being stranded or caught during a storm and in need of shelter, one must avail himself of various natural materials, and have the means to adapt them. Such materials occur in nature in many forms and differ according to the area in which they are found.

Shelter materials, like other vital means found in the natural state, are distributed throughout the world, in the Arctic, desert, forest, or swamp, and may not seem available except to the trained, observant eye. Such materials occur in various colors, grades, and forms, according to the locality.

This chapter is meant to show those unskilled and unlearned in wood lore and the ways of the wilds how to recognize and utilize these means from the vastness of nature.

When in need of cover, you will naturally have to make shelter in accordance with the situation. This may be only a simple temporary device or, in case of serious trouble, you may need to erect a permanent shelter. The latter requires considerable elaboration in selecting materials and in formulating and executing a plan. When you are forced to spend some time in one place, no effort should be spared in developing a comfortable and weatherproof shelter. This pays in a number of ways in the days to come.

The most important thing is to make the shelter rainproof; next is to make it as nearly windproof as possible. Select a campsite that will give natural drainage (a little trenching may be necessary). Do not camp in a canyon or stream bed because flash floods can be dangerous. Never camp under a lone tree, for this may serve as an electrode to draw lightning during storms. In snow country, do not make camp where snow forms drifts. And finally, always ventilate an airtight enclosure, for any type of fire gives of carbon monoxide gas, which is deadly when the oxygen content is reduced. A proper balance must be maintained between heat and air.

PARA-TEPEE

Of the many uses that a downed airman can make of his parachute, perhaps the most important is for shelter. In climates of extreme heat or cold, the para-tepee or lean-to may be vital. When a downed airman encounters wild, desolate country, he should take his parachute with him if possible. In fact, he should take all the trappings (strings, ribs, and metal parts) and as much of the fabric segments as can be carried. A number of things can be made of the parachute parts, such as snowshoes from the metal apex ribbing strips by interlacing; shelter or bedding or clothes from the nylon; sandals from the canvas bag and lashing; and fish lines and bow strings from the shroud lines. Metal parts can be heated and formed into useful implements such as fishhooks, punches, and knives. Strips of the fabric can be laid on the ground to form the letters S O S for detection by air. The parachute can make all the difference between your returning and never returning.

The para-tepee can be made from a section of parachute

covering an arrangement of poles stuck in tepee fashion. Generally, this will provide enough protection from the weather, but in extremely cold regions one should make a tepee within a tepee. This is done by erecting poles to form a somewhat larger tepee surrounding the smaller tepee. The larger one should be twelve inches wider than the other, which amounts to a six-inch air space between the two. This creates a dead-air space for insulation. The inner tepee will be many degrees warmer in the coldest weather.

An entrance is made with a pole standing against the tepee and lashed to the flap covering the entrance. Shroud lines can be used to effect this. This, in turn, is tied securely to another pole to close the door. Leave an air vent at the top, with a piece of fabric secured on a slant which permits the smoke to escape and at the same time keeps out snow or rain. In wet weather the moisture soaks into the fabric and then flows down the slanted walls and saturates it. If the tent is erected on a mound of greater diameter than the base of the tent, natural drainage will result.

LEAN-TO

A good shelter made of the parachute is the lean-to type. The edges of the shelter can be chinked in. A lean-to can be made of poles and covered by such materials as boughs, grass, bark, or moss and weighted down to stay in place. It can then be brushed in around the sides.

When sleeping in any crude shelter, you should make your bed well to insure the rest you need. Fir boughs, cattail fluff, broom sage, or Spanish moss make excellent bedding materials, for they insulate one against the cold and damp ground and are soft and comfortable to lie on.

HOGAN

The hogan, sometimes called the arch hut, is made of long, straight, switchlike poles arranged to form the walls of the hut. (See figure 23.) This is done by sticking them into holes in the ground, which are made with a sharp hardwood stick. The holes should be made in two straight lines opposite each other

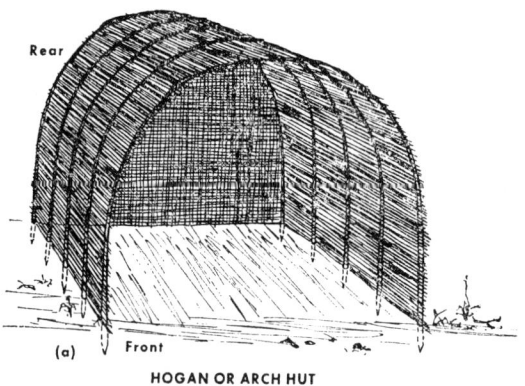

HOGAN OR ARCH HUT

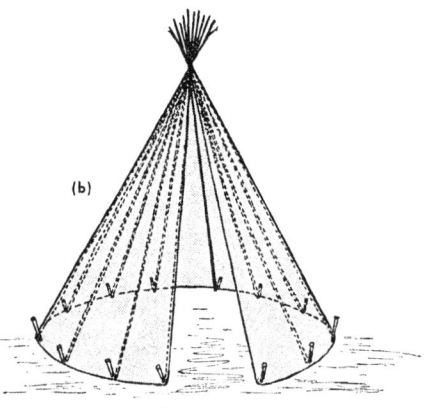

Figure 23.   Para-tepee

so that the walls are even. When the poles are inserted, they should be bent over inward and intertwined to form an arch. Another similar wall is spaced a distance of six inches from the first walls. This in effect is the same as a tepee within a tepee. The floor plan can be elongated, or the shelter can be circular.

After the set of walls is secured by tying, armfuls of broom sage, fir boughs, or other materials are packed between the two walls and across the roof. This done, tree bark or moss can be used to waterproof the roof. In the event of severe wind, the sides of the wall can be plastered with slick mud to form a daub-and-wattle wall. This was often used by Indian tribes in North America.

ADOBE

When the need arises for a more permanent shelter, a very serviceable and weatherproof sort is made with adobe or other clay, which is plentiful in many parts of the continent. If clay of the more common type is used, a tough, wiry straw should be mixed with it in order to hold the bricks together in bad weather.

To build the house, first make large bricks by digging a shallow pit and mixing water with the clay to a stiff consistency. The clay is now molded into bricks of about six by six by twelve inches. When a number of bricks are formed and dried in the sun and wind, they can be used as molds for forming more bricks by arranging them in one-layer checkerboard fashion, leaving out every other brick. More bricks are made by filling the blank spaces with clay and allowing them to dry. They are easily separated when sufficiently dry, but must be dried further in the sun so as to harden and temper. Repeat this method until you have the required number. Always give the bricks a final sunning after taking them from the mold.

The shoulder blade of a large deerlike animal serves well as a shovel, a mixer, and a trowel for spreading mortar between bricks. The unmortared bricks should be spaced out accurately to obtain proper spacing of joints from corner to corner. This insures the forming of clean, precise corners and door and window openings. If you maintain the same mortar thickness of the bonds, you will have walls of uniform height.

A nearly flat roof can be formed of poles and thin brick, then covered with sod. A slightly sloped roof provides ample drainage. Windows can be of oiled fishskins or animal skins. These keep out the weather and admit some light.

Adobe huts are cool in the desert heat and warm in winter.

CAVES

Caves are nature-made or they can be man-made, and are welcome refuges in bad weather. A traveler is fortunate indeed to stumble upon one at such times or when in need of rest. The temperature of a cave is fairly even the year round. While they are moderately cool in the summer, they are comfortably warm in winter if there is no draft. Many, especially limestone caves, contain cold water springs or lakelets which almost certainly are fit for drinking.

Man-made caves, such as those in clay banks or snow drifts to provide protection from intense heat or cold, can be made almost anywhere.

Insect pests are of little consequence in a cave, and blow flies are not apt to discover fresh meat hanging there. A cave is of definite advantage over most emergency shelters and should not be passed up in time of need.

Snow caves are simply cave-like excavations in the lee side of a snowdrift which has banked against some obstruction,

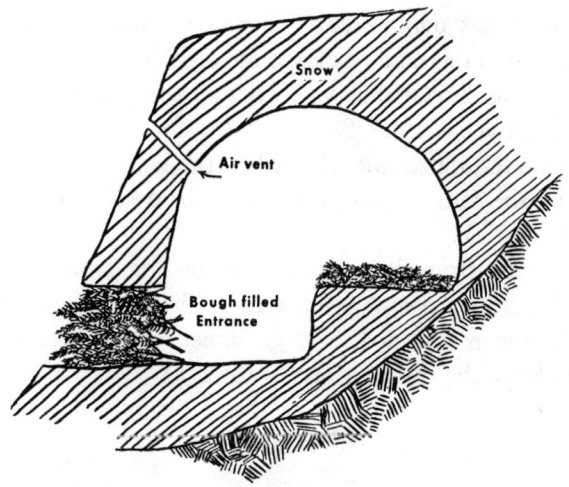

Figure 24. SNOWDRIFT SHELTER (cave)

such as a low-spreading fir tree, and affords protection against severely cold winds. (See figure 24.) A tiny fire or grease lamp can be used in a snow cave, provided plenty of air is admitted for ventilation. The floor can be carpeted with fir boughs.

Ice houses or Eskimo-type huts can be made of blocks of ice stacked in a domelike enclosure, which is amply heated by grease lamps.

Small caves are ideal in combating desert heat during the daytime. One can dig a slit trench, running with the wind if possible, but always crosswise to the path of the sun; and it should be shaded by brush with green foliage, to shield it from the torrid, sun-parched desert. Inside, a person should move about as little as necessary to conserve body moisture and energy, and he should do most of his traveling at night and early and late in the day. A considerable distance can be traversed on a moonlit night. If he travels too much during the heat of the day, he will be subject to dehydration.

Research has demonstrated that desert animals survive by tunneling into the sand to escape the terrible heat by day.

Tests have shown that when the air temperature is 115°, the sand surface is 150° F.

It is interesting to note that when the sand at the surface is 150° F., the temperature at 6 inches below is 74.5° and at 18 inches 61° F.

Protection from heat, so important for animals, means protection from the sun's temperature. The best solution for the animal, human included, is to go underground, because there he can escape the burning rays of the sun.

12
Transportation

In most cases, a person who gets separated from his party or lost will eventually be able to find his way home or to his base of operations. But when the situation is more serious, as when one's plane crashes or he is otherwise stranded, certain things can be done to facilitate a return to safety. Passengers may have sustained serious injury or illness, and a good mode of transportation is imperative to survival. Boats or other conveyances are a good means of traveling, and rivers are the wilderness highways. To follow a stream either afloat or afoot is usually the best route to civilization.

BOATS

A frame of light stout willow poles, fashioned in the shape of a boat, can be covered with a waterproof tarpaulin to provide a makeshift craft. In using something of this kind, be on the lookout for sharp snags and rocks lest they puncture the craft. Also, one can make a similar boat with bags of cattail fluff. Sealed tin cans may be substituted, and can be used as life preservers. Joints of bamboo can be used in the same way.

One should stay close to the edge when crossing a large lake because high winds may develop which could capsize the boat.

A floating craft can be made of dry bamboo poles by reversing the ends of half the number and keeping the switch ends pointed towards the ends of the craft. The number of canes required is determined by the extent of the load. Probably four or five hundred canes are needed to float two persons of ordinary size. These canes should be at least twelve feet long and of the type found in rich river bottoms.

The mid-section of the craft should be the overlapping butt ends of the canes, which are securely tied together. The craft should be made in a troughlike shape. The end switches must be tied together to a point. An outrigger can be employed. This is done by securing a pole crossways to the craft at each end and extending a few feet from the craft. Now a light log several inches in diameter should be tied to these and parallel with the craft, to prevent capsizing.

A mast pole and sail can be erected by striking the mast pole in the center of the craft. A bush top-heavy witth foliage may be substituted for the mast and pole, to help carry a person to his destination more swiftly in a good breeze.

The construction and use of a log raft is generally known, so there is no need to go into it.

CANOE

In the past, canoes were highly prized by the Indians of northern United States and Canada. Portions of birch bark can be procured with care. Frames for the canoe should be made of branches from such trees as elm, birch, or willow.

In fitting the bark slabs in place, hold two sections together and mark the layout of holes for sewing or lacing so that they match both pieces. The holes should be of the same diameter. Rawhide strips or thongs should be larger than the holes so as to fit snugly, and they should be saturated in oil, fat, or tallow before stitching, to insure that water does not seep through. To obtain uniformity of size for the holes, use a fire-hardened piece of pointed hardwood with a shoulder for a depth stop, like a simple depth gauge.

When the canoe is fully laced up, resin or pitch of fir, spruce, or tamarack should be heated to a liquid state and applied to seams and holes. This further insures against leakage. These should be pitched within and without. A good supply of resinous pitch should be taken along while canoeing in case repairs are necessary.

ESKIMO BOATS

Eskimo boats can be made of skins stretched over frames, similar to a canoe, but fully covered except where the paddler sits. The kind intended for one occupant is called a kayak; a larger type, used by several, is called an umiak. Kayaks are used principally for hunting seals and for fishing. The umiak is suitable also for traveling.

DUGOUT

Now suppose you are lost in the northwoods or in some jungle country and you need a boat for getting food or for returning to some civilized spot. If you possessed an ax it would be all the better, but even if you don't, you can still make a boat. With fire, you can burn down a tree, or perhaps there is already a suitable log available for making a dugout canoe. The Indians used to burn down a tree of the desired length, then burn away by means of small, controlled fires all the excess interior wood. Thus the log is hollowed out in time, and with perseverance and patience you can fashion a useful dugout. The charred embers are removed with sharp stones or clam shells. Often this type of boat can be propelled without paddles or oars simply by using a pushpole. An outrigger is worth adding to prevent capsizing.

While traveling by boat, you can save time by cooking on board, avoiding the need to stop at intervals to make camp along the shore. This is done by making a small hearth of clay in the boat. The fire will be a luxury, giving warmth on cold days or nights.

On swift streams keep a sharp vigil for treacherous rapids or waterfalls. In the event the boat capsizes, stay with the boat —it is buoyant and may be your best chance of reaching land.

During storms, a boat can be used as a windbreak by hauling it ashore and turning it bottom up. A forked stick will serve to hold a side upright so that you may crawl under it for shelter. The lee side should be raised. In the case of rain, put the boat so as to take advantage of natural drainage, but even then a little trenching may be necessary. When a boat is used in this manner during a snowstorm, it should be brushed in with boughs or other materials. Bear in mind also that your boat can be turned over and be used for a table or work bench.

TRAVOIS

This was used by American Indians during frontier days. It got its name from the French explorers. It is a simple and crude contrivance requiring little mechanical ability to make. However crude, it serves a useful purpose.

There are two kinds of travois, those drawn by animals—horses, camels, llamas, and dogs—and the other which is drawn by man. That drawn by animals is simply a pair of long, slender poles of equal lengths (usually seasoned for lightness), one secured to each side of the beast by means of a simple collar which fits around the base of the animal's neck. A leather strap is thrown across the animal's back, each end secured to a pole; the other ends slant down and drag on the ground. The load is placed to the rear of the animal, couch-fashioned or on crosspiece. Such a contraption can be used, among other things, to transport an injured, sick, or otherwise immobilized person.

The man-drawn travois is made by selecting a small sapling or bush with a hook limb and a long forked switch top. When all the other limbs are trimmed off, the hook limb is cut to a length of about two feet. This must be at right angles to the fork, as the hook is to fit over the shoulder while the fork lies flat on the ground. The switch fork takes a gradual curve from the man's shoulder and down to the ground to form a sledlike arrangement. New crosspieces should be tied to the fork to form a crude platform. An injured person can be transported in this manner. Also, it facilitates bringing big game back to camp. This method keeps a deer down low out of the view of other hunters, reducing the risk of being shot at.

TOBOGGAN

Toboggans or sleds may be the only answer to one's needs in case a sick or injured person has to be moved, or when transporting camp gear.

Sleds can be built by hewing crude runners from a slender birch sapling. The runners are steamed over hot coals of an open fire and the forward ends bent into a curved shape to slide over ice and snow. The proper curvatures are obtained by bending and weighting them into the desired shape with some heavy object—stones or logs, or they may be formed with rope and forked stick. This is accomplished by tying a rope to the front end of the runner and to the middle part. A forked stick is set to spring an arch curve between the rope and the runner, by setting it at right angles to the rope and runner. The runners must be curved alike to run true, and seasoned to prevent sticking. The more polish one can get on the undersides, the easier they slide. Hot tree resin or tallow applied to the underside from time to time adds to gliding capability.

The runners should be spaced and braced with crosspieces, by making two holes side by side an inch apart and located near each end of the runners. A deep notch at the underside and directly beneath the two holes for the lashings secures the crosspieces so that they are raised above the ice. The center point of the X of the crosspieces should be firmly secured to form a fixed brace between the runners.

It requires only a little more work to construct a pair of sides and a seat on top of the crosspieces.

TRAVEL BY WATER

In paddling, you can do it in such a way as to keep the canoe on a straight course. You must pull the paddle straight back for three-quarters of the stroke, then abruptly swing the paddle out and away from the boat in a sweeping arc. This counteracts the tendency of the canoe to nose to the opposite side. Always paddle from one side of the boat only; don't alternate sides.

When encountering waves, always quarter the waves by moving the boat to nose across them at a forty-five-degree angle. Don't head into the large waves, and never let the waves catch you broadsides, as this will almost certainly capsize the craft.

Crossing streams may present special problems when returning home. A stout pole furnishes good support in crossing shallow, swift streams. It can also be used to feel for a sudden drop-off or pocket. Keeping your body low will take most of the weight off your feet and thus reduce danger from bruises. In crossing a stream, take a diagonal course; do not fight the current. Going downstream, try to stay on the inside of the current, where it is usually not as swift and the stream is often shallower. Try to keep your body horizontal with the stream to reduce the chance of being pulled under. Go on your back feet first down fast-moving rapids. Go head first and on your belly down deep water. Keep as near to shore as possible and watch out for waterfalls and white water. Backwater eddys and converging currents often make dangerous swirls. Bubbling water, as found below waterfalls and rapids, is less buoyant.

Don't take chances swimming in cold water or soon after eating, because cramps may develop.

When crossing swamp bogs, quicksands, or undependable ice-covered streams, always carry a rope extended from person to person and keep scattered out somewhat so as to distribute weight. It is a good idea to carry a light pole across the shoulder at such places; you will then have something to climb out on in case of emergency. If you break through thin ice, place your hands on the ice and then kick your feet until your body is level with the ice and then swim onto the ice. From there you can crawl to a safe place. Don't try to stand up.

A shirt can be made buoyant by buttoning all but the top button and then breathing air into the wet shirt. Also, if your trousers are cotton, they can be made buoyant by removing them and tying knots in the legs, then quickly pull the open top end down to submerge everything. Air is thus trapped in the legs, acting as a life preserver.

JELLYFISH FLOAT

If you have fallen overboard or have a long way to swim, you may be able to rest at intervals and remain afloat for about two days if you know how. Simply fill your lungs with air and double up with your arms clasping your knees, stay partly submerged until you have to come up for air. Repeat this until rested, then resume swimming in various ways. Back or side stroke is easiest and will help you to endure. Float jellyfish fashion whenever you get tired. Frog float is equally effective. Simply spread arms and legs, face down, and you will float.

13
Trapping

Throughout the ages trapping has played an important part in securing wild game, both for meat and for skins. There are many other things for which the carcass of an animal can be used. Birds and fish also have been taken in great numbers by trapping.

TRAPS AND SNARES

Traps are any sort of device that catches and holds unwary game. It may be a cage with a trap door, a log deadfall, a pitfall, a steel trap, a net, or a simple string snare.

Trapping, more often than not, means spending a lot of time walking considerable distances from camp, but generally it is a very cheap and effective means of securing game.

In trapping certain animals, care must be exercised in selecting the spot where it is most likely to score a catch; also, you must take care to leave no scent or trace of yourself. Some trap sets require only a set with bait to catch the more gullible animals.

Trapping has, in certain respects, advantages over hunting. A hunter has to venture out to his game, whereas the game comes to the trapper who is clever enough to set and manage

FLAT STONE TRAP

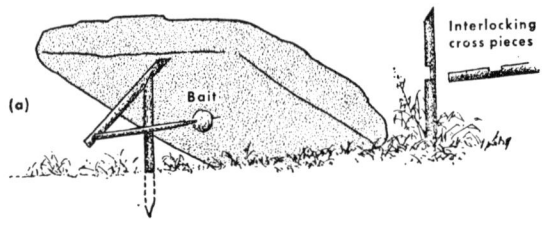

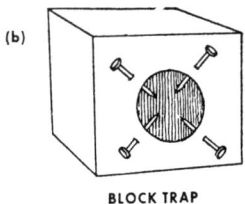

BLOCK TRAP   Figure 25.

his line strategically. A hunter may exhaust his supply of ammunition, but all a trapper needs to keep going is his ax and knife. Trapping, like hunting or fishing, is no lazy man's game, and to be successful one must work constantly and efficiently.

When faced with the problem of survival, trapping in its most elementary form may be the only means of securing game —the use of some simple device such as a deadfall or snare. At any rate, if it doesn't provide the main source of food it will surely supplement other means of obtaining something to eat; so when in distress, don't overlook any means of obtaining food and other materials which supply a need. With a little imagination one may find uses for practically every part of an animal, bird, or fish.

In the wild areas one should carry a supply of rawhide strings about six feet long, for, besides using them for snares,

Trapping / 143

they can serve numerous other purposes (See figures 25 and 26, deadfalls and snares.)

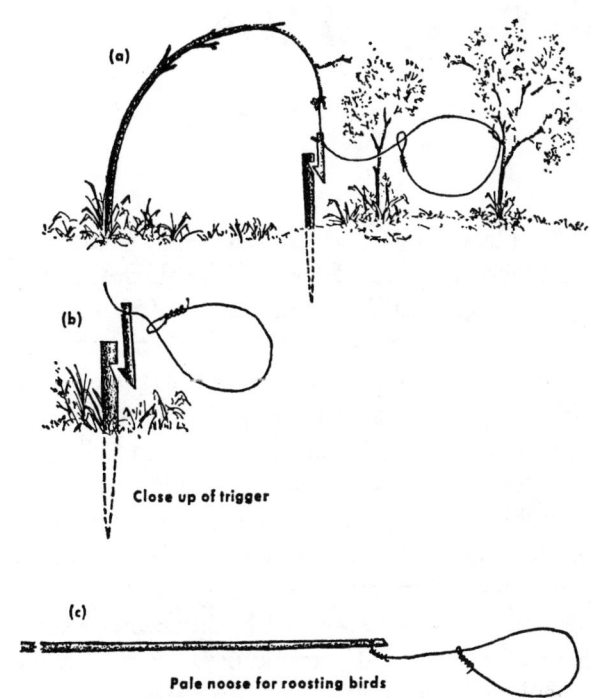

Figure 26. RABBIT RUN SNARE

14
The Survival Kit

Shipwreck, plane crash, and car failure are common causes which occasion the need of the individual, the family, or a group to live temporarily off the land. Work or play in a remote area, such as prospecting, timber cruising, camping, hiking, hunting, fishing, and trapping can isolate a person in the wilderness. Local catastrophe, including flood, fire, and blizzard create a survival problem for people of all ages, most of whom depend upon others for help. Electrical failure can be responsible for similar hardships in a community. Then there is the ugly specter of war clouds with the threat of national catastrophe. Survival is an aftermath of bombings, hand in hand with resistance to invasion by an enemy. Hence, there is both practical need and patriotic need for preparedness. In such a case knowledge is vital to preparedness.

In the event of accident, one should, when in a crash or stranded, strip his aircraft, boat, or car of the things which can be converted into useful articles. Some things conceivably useful are: mirrors and metal pieces, gasoline and oil, radiator water free of anti-freeze fluid, and wires. These and other objects may be enlisted into valuable service. There are signals, as with mirrors, for attracting attention, and fuel for signal fires. Wires can be used for lashings or fish lines. Clear radiator water can be drunk, although it may first require filtering. Tires can be broken down and used in various ways. The nylon lining cords may prove valuable, and the wires at the rim of tires can be used for shelter lashings or animal and fish snares. Tire rubber can be cut up into sandals.

Preparation can alleviate any emergency or catastrophe. Preparedness to meet the challenge of survival on the part of humans can be likened unto nature's law of the survival of the fittest with all forms of life. By having in readiness a portable survival kit and knowing how to use its contents, man can fit himself to prevail against all odds.

The kit can be carried aboard any sort of craft, canoe or yacht. Attached to the CO_2 cartridge-type life preserver, it can be made to float in an emergency and it can support a person along with the kit. It can be included on horseback trail or on portage. It should always be a part of camping equipment, especially in a remote region. The survival kit is the outdoor person's life assurance and insurance; it is his policy, plan and equipment. It should be instantly available.

The starting point is the container. One or two aluminum boxes, with handle and hinged-clamp fasteners made expressly for carrying roller skates to and from the rink, is ideal. After packing, they can be sealed so as to be waterproof, dustproof, and to a degree fireproof. Once packed, tape can be wrapped around the division between lid and box then painted with quick-drying enamel.

To a certain extent, contents are a matter of personal choice, depending upon need and preference. It might feature supplies for a frigid environment or for an arid desert. Nevertheless, a list is necessary. The following is suggested:

CHECK LIST

Hardware and Dry Goods

Note pad and pencil for map sketching.

Two sturdy pocket knives, with several blades.
Hunting knife with six-inch blade, plus file and knife hone.
Compass.
Magnifying glass in leather case.
Two signal mirrors of the metal type (military).
Two waterproofed plastic boxes or jars of waterproofed matches.
One light hatchet head (handle can be cut later).
Card of needles and thread.
Card of large safety pins.
Supply of rawhide laces.
Bandanna for head and neck gear.
Several lamp wicks.
One plumber's candle.
Roll of aluminum cooking foil.
Revolver, .22 caliber, and 500 rounds of ammunition.

Foods

One pound of salt in jar.
One pound of sugar cubes in plastic container.
Instant coffee and/or tea in jar.
Powdered milk in jar.
Dehydrated soup packed in frying pan.
Dehydrated fruit packed in cooking pot.
Assorted shelled nuts and concentrated chocolate candy packed in coffee pot.
Dehydrated meat, such as salted fish and dried beef.
Canned beef and sardines.
   Cheese in plastic container.
Pint jar of honey for sugar energy.

Hunting and Fishing Equipment

Coil of wire for snares.
Two bow strings of 65-pound pull.
One sturdy fish gig.
One flat steel spear blade.
Packet of flat steel arrowheads, 2 doz. or more.
Fishhooks, eyed-100 #6, 100 #2, 100 #12.
100 yards of 36-lb. braided nylon.
100 yards of 15-lb. monofilament.
Assortment of artificial flies, worms, spinners and spoons.
Six or more ounces of rotenone fish killer.

First Aid

First Aid Kit including large roll of adhesive tape, two packs of bandages and gauze, salve, 4 oz. of 7% tincture of iodine for disinfectant and for purifying water and chlorine tablets for same purpose. One doz. quart-size plastic bags for canteen substitute and for purifying water chemically. Snakebite kit with tourniquet. Insect repellent including sulphur candles.

FIREARMS

It is wise to carry a rifle. A .22 caliber with open iron sights is best all-round firearm to carry in the car, boat, or plane, or to have in the wilds. One can pack a good supply of .22 long rifle cartridges for distance shooting and a large supply of .22 shorts for quiet close-up work. The lightness and smallness of the gun and the smallness and cheapness of the ammunition are advantages. This little weapon can be used to secure food, signal for help, and for self-protection. A one-cent shot can kill a deer.

All parts of the gun should be cleaned and flushed with oil. A hole about four-fifths of an inch in diameter and four inches in depth can be drilled into the stock after the butt plate has been removed. This serves as a storage place for matches and salt. A glassine envelope of salt can be wrapped around waterproofed matches. A cork, cut to fit, seals the hole, and the butt plate is put back as before. This is additional security, particularly for hunters, against a night in the wilds.

The rifle can be strapped or taped to the survival kit, thus becoming a part of it. Thus the revolver could be omitted from the check list. By the same token, it would be fine to add a hand ax or machete and omit the hatchet head.

Index

Amebae, 37
Antivenin, 26
Aquatic animals, 101–2

Bacilli, 26
Bamboo, 116
Bark, 109–10
Basketry, 82
Beaded Lizard, 27
Beverages from plants, 109
Birds, 100–1
Blanching, 124
Bleeding, 35
Blind, 97
Blisters, 30, 33
Blow flies, 123
Boats, 133–36
Bola, 77–78
Bone marrow, 98
Boomerang, 78
Bow and arrow, 73–76
Bread, 119–20
Burns, 33–34

Canoe, 134–35
Canteen, 79
Cattail, 30, 111
Caves, 130
Check list, 145–48
Chitterlings, 98
Clay, 129–30
Coconut, 114
Compass, 42
Cooking, 115–24
Copperheads, 27
Coral snake, 24, 27

Cream of tartar tablets, 28
Crustaceans, 102–3, 120

Diarrhea, 29
Dugout, 135–36
Dysentery, 29

Epsom salts, 27

Fainting, 36
Fat, 99
Fever, 30
Fibers, 111, 114
Firearm, 147–48
Firemaking, 60–70
First aid, 20–21, 147
Fishing equipment, 88–95
Fractures, 31
Frogs, 104
Frostbite, 34–35
Fruits, 108–9

Gila monster, 27

Hand drill, 72
Heart attack, 22–24
Heatstroke, 32
Hemotoxic, 26
Hides, 86–88
Hobo stove, 122
Hogan, 128–29

Implementation, 71–95
Insects, 28, 38
Iodine, 26

Jerky, 123

Large game, 96–98
Lean-to, 127
Ligature, 26
Lye, 28

Mollusks, 102
Mushrooms, 105–8

Neurotoxic, 26

Orientation, 39
Oysters, 102–3

Palms, 113
Pitch, 135
Plants, 105–14
Poisonous plants, 29
Pottery, 82–84

Quarter staff, 79–80

Rattlesnake, 27, 38
Resuscitation, 22–23
Roots, 109–10

Salt, 110, 114, 122, 124
Sand shelter, 132
Scurvy, 30
Shellfish, 101–2
Shelter, 125–32
Shock, 27, 36
Signaling, 45
Small game, 98–100
Smoked meat and fish, 123
Snakebite, 24–27

Snakebite kits, 27
Snares, 141–43
Snow blindness, 80
Snowdrift shelter, 131
Snowshoes, 81
Soapmaking, 85, 113
Spear, 76–77, 90–91
Special plants, 111–114
Sprains, 31
Stars, 40–41
Starvation, 110
Sugar, 122
Sulphur, 28
Sunstroke, 32
Survival kit, 144–48

Tannic acid, 29
Tepee, 126–27
Tetanus, 26
Toboggan, 137–38
Tourniquet, 26
Toxicity, 114
Transportation, 133–40
Trapping, 141–43
Travois, 31, 136–37
Turtles, 103–4, 120
Twist stick, 99

Venom, 24, 26, 28

Water, 49–59
Water moccasin, 27
Wild grains, 108–9

Yucca, 112